TOWER SERIES   NUMBER SEVEN

The Poet's Vocation

The Poet's

from letters of HÖLDERLIN,

Edited & translated by WILLIAM BURFORD

with drawings by CYRIL SATORSKY

Vocation : Selections

RIMBAUD & HART CRANE

and CHRISTOPHER MIDDLETON

THE UNIVERSITY OF TEXAS

Permission to reprint the selections from the letters of Hart Crane is gratefully acknowledged to Samuel Loveman, Executor of the Hart Crane Estate

Second Impression

Library of Congress Catalogue Card Number : 62–62940

Published by
HUMANITIES RESEARCH CENTER, THE UNIVERSITY OF TEXAS

Distributed by
UNIVERSITY OF TEXAS PRESS, *Austin, Texas 78712*

Printed and bound in the United States of America

FOREWORD

"There is no great expedition, in art, which is not under-taken at peril of one's life," the French poet, André Breton, has written. For the poets whose letters are brought to-gether here—Hölderlin, Rimbaud, Hart Crane—this state-ment of Breton's especially holds true. None of the three wished in some romantic fashion of poetic behaviour, will-fully to put his life in peril; on the contrary, all were seek-ing happiness, joy, and abundant existence; all were fighters in an instinctive human way; but their desires assumed such an absolute form and their search led them to such a pitch of imaginary conception, of which their poetry is the record, as these letters also are, that their vocation did, indeed, ul-timately lead them into peril. They were absolutists in their lives and in the writing of their poems. In an essay on his first published volume, 'White Buildings,' Hart Crane rec-ognized the poet's absolutism and defined it quite clearly, a definition that may serve for Hölderlin and Rimbaud as well.

"It may not be possible to say that there is, strictly speak-ing, any 'absolute' experience. But it seems evident that cer-tain aesthetic experience (and this may for a time engross the total faculties of the spectator) can be called absolute, inasmuch as it approximates a formally convincing state-ment of a conception or apprehension of life that gains our unquestioning assent . . ."

There is a point for such a poet, at least, at which his role of participant in his own work increasingly predominates over his role as spectator of it; at which he requires that the practices of art and of daily life join together, a point at which the making of the poem and the making of his life must be virtually the same. This might be called the point of peril; for what is formally convincing and gains unquestion-ing assent in the poem may not be possible in life; the poem and the life may drastically diverge. When Crane said, "it is part of a poet's business to risk not only criticism—but folly—in the conquest of consciousness," he probably real-ised that he was referring not only to poetry but also to life,

5

but he probably did not quite recognise that the triumph of folly in the poem, accompanied as it is in a great poem also by the triumph of conscious artistry, could hardly be duplicated in the poet's actual life, which cannot be so formally controlled as the poem is. The letters selected here may be read as a testament to three great expeditions in art and in life, always perilous for the absolutist, but always necessary to him.

WILLIAM BURFORD
CHRISTOPHER MIDDLETON

The Hölderlin section of this book is the work of Christopher Middleton; the sections devoted to Rimbaud and Hart Crane are the work of William Burford.

The letters of

HÖLDE IN

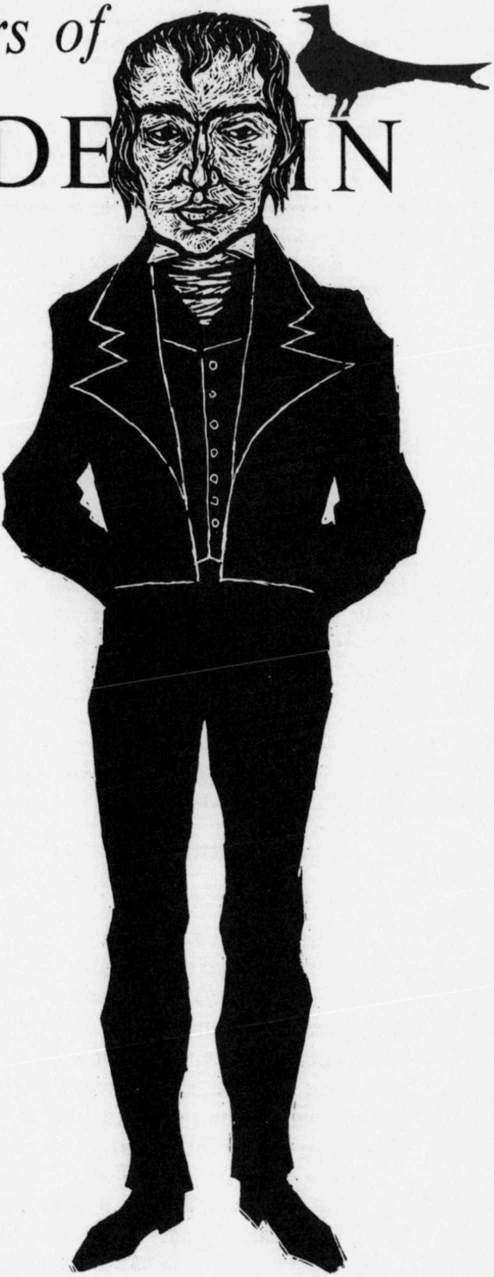

*There are 313 letters in Volume VI (1954) of Hölderlin's works
in the "Grosse Stuttgarter Ausgabe". Of these, 247 are dated
1785–1804. The rest, mainly polite notes to his mother, dated
1806–28, were written when the poet was mad. The letters
selected were all written between his twenty-fourth and thirty-
second year (1794–1802), the eight years of his sane maturity.
For much of this time, Hölderlin earned his living as a private
tutor. He earned little from his writings; but his mother helped
him from time to time as best she could. He appears as a deeply
pensive young man, immersed in philosophical and Greek
studies, but also as a childlike nature, self-centered but seldom
self-possessed. A diffuseness, turbid at points, in his off-hand
writing, makes one marvel all the more at the craftsmanship
and lucidity of his poems. English can hardly be persuaded to
recreate his peculiarities of style and tone, the involved periods,
the solemnity. But the attempt has been made to follow Hölderlin here, as in his diction. The diction, again, is peculiar.
Hölderlin gives recurrent words, consistently, a dimension of
meaning which they did not have in the usage of his time. His
own usage injects special meanings even into common words,
like* Ruhe; *more complex words, like* Popularität *in the second
letter to Böhlendorff, do face the translator with problems.
These letters of 1794–1802 are so much concerned with ideas,
that the reader might wonder what has become of the sublunary
things of life (in which Keats, by contrast, was much absorbed).
But Hölderlin's age was, after all, dominated by ideas. Also the
objects of his provincial world were already familiar enough to
his correspondents. Hölderlin's mature poetry dwells lovingly,
it is true, on sublunary things. But the orientation of his letters,
like those by many of his contemporaries, is naturally abstract.*

To CHRISTIAN LUDWIG NEUFFER
JENA, NOVEMBER 1794.[1]

. . . My head and heart are full now of the things that I want
to do, thinking and writing, also in action, as duty, not only
the last, of course. The nearness of truly great minds, also of
truly great, independent and energetic hearts, depresses and
elates me alternately, I must help myself out from twilight
and sleep, I must gently exert myself to arouse and shape
half-grown and half-dead faculties in myself, if I am not in
the end to escape into a sad resignation, where one consoles

[1] Neuffer (1769–1839) had first met Hölderlin at the Tübingen theological seminary (Tübinger Stift) during the winter
1788–89. They corresponded regularly from 1788 to 1800.

10

oneself with other unripe and powerless beings, lets the world run its course, with the falling and rising of truth and justice, the flowering and dying of art, the death and life of all that interests man as man, where one contemplates all this calmly from one's corner, and, when a crisis comes, confronts the demands of humanity with one's negative virtue. Better the grave than such a state. And yet I often have almost nothing else in view. Dear old friend, in such moments I really do miss your company, your comfort, and the visible example of your steadfastness. I know that sometimes you, too, lose courage, I know that it is the general fate of souls which have more than animal needs; it is just that the degrees are different. A remark which I happened to see today in the announcement of Wieland's collected works is still burning in my heart. It says: "Wieland's Muse began with the beginning of German poetry and will end only when it ends." I ask you. Call me a fool, but a thing like this can spoil a whole week for me. All right, if it must be so, then let us smash our miserable harps and act—as the artists dreamed of doing. That's my comfort. —Now some details about this place. At present, Fichte is the soul of Jena. And thank God that he is. I know no man with such depth and energy of mind; to seek and define, in the farthest regions of human knowledge, the principles of this knowledge, and with them the principles of justice, and to think out with the same intellectual power from these principles the farthest and most daring consequences, and despite the power of darkness to write them down and to speak on them, with a fire and precision whose union would have seemed perhaps an insoluble problem to poor me, without this example,—this, dear Neuffer, is most certainly something, and it is certainly not saying too much of this man. I hear his lectures every day. Talk with him sometimes. I've already visited Schiller a few times, the first time not exactly with success. I went in, got a friendly welcome, and hardly noticed in the background a stranger of whom not a gesture and for long afterward not a sound made me suspect anything special. Schiller introduced us, but I did not gather his name. Coldly, almost without a glance, I said How-do-you-do, and was altogether occupied with Schiller, inwardly and outwardly; the stranger did not say anything for a long time. Schiller brought the issue of *Thalia* which contained a frag-

11

ment of my *Hyperion* and my poem 'To Destiny', and gave it to me. Since Schiller then left the room for a moment, the stranger picked up the journal from the table by me, thumbed through the fragment, standing by my side, and said nothing. I felt myself blushing all over. Had I known what I know now, I would have gone as pale as a corpse. Then he turned to me, asked after Frau von Kalb, about the whereabouts and neighbors of our village, and I answered rather more monosyllabically than is perhaps my usual way. But it was just my unlucky day. Schiller came back, we talked about the theater in Weimar, the stranger made a few casual remarks, which were weighty enough to make me suspect something. But I suspected nothing. Maier, the painter from Weimar, also came. The stranger spoke with him about various things. But I suspected nothing. I left, and heard on the same day in the Professors' Club—what do you think?—that Goethe had been with Schiller this noon.

Heaven help me to make good my misfortune and foolishness when I get to Weimar. Afterward, I had supper with Schiller and he consoled me as best he could, also with his serenity; and his conversation, in which his whole colossal mind displayed itself, made me forget my ill-luck at the earlier visit . . .

Hölderlin spent six months in Jena from November 1794, with Schiller and Fichte as his chief mentors. Yet he soon became critical of Fichte's thinking. He found Schelling's ideas more congenial, after 1797; and his theory of organicity in poetry, sketched in the letter to Neuffer dated July 3, 1799, does have features in common with the organicity theory advanced in Schelling's Ideen zu einer Philosophie der Natur (1797), a book which Coleridge also adopted. Hölderlin's attention to the philosophical thought of his time, the new Idealism, was matched by his concern with the social and political consequences of the French Revolution. The latter had meant the beginning of a new era of social freedom; and the new philosophy was among the tokens of what Hölderlin called in 1797 a "coming revolution in ways of thinking." Early in 1796, a change had affected his own life. In January he became private tutor in the house of a Frankfurt business man, Jakob Friedrich Gontard (1764–1843); soon he was deeply in love with his employer's wife, Susette, who became the "Diotima" of his poems and of his novel "Hyperion". From this period dates his first mature work.

I know that it is infinitely painful to leave a place where one has seen all the fruits and flowers of humanity burgeoning in one's hopes. Yet one has oneself, and a few individuals; and it is also good to find, in oneself and a few individuals, a world.

As for things in general, I do find one consolation, which is that that ferment and dissolution must lead either to annihilation or to re-organization.[1] But there is no such thing as annihilation, so the youth of the world must return, out of our decay. Surely one can say without a doubt that there were never before so many things afoot in the world. It is a gigantic multiplicity of contradictions and contrasts. Old and new. Culture and crudity. Wickedness and passion. Egoism in sheep's clothing, egoism in wolf's clothing. Superstition and unbelief. Slavery and despotism. Unreasoning cleverness, unclever reason. Mindless sensibility, insensitive mind. History and experience and tradition without philosophy, philosophy without experience. Energy without principles, principles without energy. Severity without loving kindness, loving kindness without severity. Hypocritical complacency, shameless impertinence. Precocious boys, idiotic men. —The litany could go on from sunrise to midnight and still have named hardly a thousandth part of the human chaos. But so it should be. This character of the better-known sector of the human race is certainly a forecast of extraordinary things to come. I believe in a coming revolution of attitudes and of ways of thinking, which will make everything till now blush for shame. And perhaps Germany can contribute to this. The more quietly a state grows, the more glorious is its maturity. Germany is quiet, modest, men are thinking much, working much, and in the hearts of young men there are stirrings which do not overflow in empty phrases as elsewhere. Much cultivation of the mind, and, infinitely more important, the right raw material—good temperedness and industry, childlikeness of heart and virility of mind, these are the elements from which an excellent people shapes and cultivates itself.

[1] The French Revolution was in its eighth year.

I have sailed around a world of joy since last we wrote to each other. I would gladly have told you about myself before, had I ever stood still and looked back. The wave carried me onward; my whole being was always too deeply immersed in life to reflect upon itself.

And it is still like this, I am still as happy as in the first moment. It is an eternal, happy, holy friendship with a being who has simply strayed into this poor, spiritless and disordered century. My sense of beauty is now secure against disturbance. It takes its orientation eternally from this madonna's head. My understanding goes to school with her, and my discordant heart is daily calmed and cheered within her contented peace. I can tell you, dear Neuffer, that I am on my way to becoming a very good boy. And in other ways, too, I am a little more satisfied with myself. I write little and philosophize hardly at all now. But what I do write has more vitality and shape; my imagination is more willingly receptive to everyday things; my heart is full of delight; and if holy destiny keeps my lucky life intact, I hope to do more than I have done till now.

. . .

I wanted to write you such a long letter, good Neuffer, but the poor moments that I have are too few for me now to tell you what has seized me and dwells in me. Besides, it always kills our quiet bliss to be turned into speech. I prefer simply to go on, in happy and lovely peace, like a child, without counting what I have and am, for no thought can wholly comprehend what I do have. But I would like to show you her image, then there would be no more need for words. She is beautiful, like angels. A delicate, spiritual, heavenly-charming face. I could forget myself and everything for a thousand years in blissful contemplation, with her, so inexhaustibly rich in this image is this quiet unassuming soul. Majesty and delicacy, and serenity and seriousness and sweet playfulness and lofty sorrow and life and spirit; in and upon her being all things conjoin in a single divine whole. Good night, dear friend. "To him, whom the gods love, is given great joy, great sorrow." There is no art in sailing down the stream. But when heart and destiny hurl us down to the sea's floor and up into the heavens, that trains the helmsman.

14

In September 1798, Hölderlin had to leave the Gontard house-hold. He spent the next fifteen months in Homburg von der Hohe, near Frankfurt. It was a productive time for him. He was also developing the poetics upon which his poems hereafter are based.

To NEUFFER   *HOMBURG, NOVEMBER 12, 1798.*
. . .

Livingness in poetry is what now most preoccupies my mind and senses. I feel so deeply how far I am from attaining it, and yet my whole soul is struggling to do so, and often I am so overcome that I weep like a child when I feel in every way the lack in my work of one thing or another, and still I cannot wrest myself off the wrong poetic tracks on which I wander around. O the world has scared my mind back into itself ever since my youth, and I am still suffering from this. There is, to be sure, one honorable refuge for a poet who comes to grief like me: philosophy. But I cannot relinquish my first love and the hopes of my young days, and I would rather perish with nothing done than leave the sweet land of the Muses, out of which only chance has driven me. If you have any good advice, which would bring me to the truth as quickly as possible, then give it to me. I lack not so much power as ease, not so much ideas as nuances, not so much a fundamental tone as variously patterned tones, not so much light as shadows, and all this for one single reason: I am too shy of what is common and ordinary in actual life. I am a proper pedant, if you like. And yet, unless I am mistaken, pedants are so cold and loveless, whereas my heart is so impatient to ally itself with sublunary people and things. I almost think that I am pedantic out of sheer love, I am not shy because I am afraid of being disturbed by reality in my self-absorbtion, but because I am afraid of being disturbed by reality in the inward communion with which I gladly attach myself to something else; I am afraid to chill the warm life in me with the icy history of common day, and this fear springs from my having been more sensitively receptive than others to any destructive thing which befell me, ever since my youth, and this sensitivity seems to be rooted in my being not firmly and indestructibly organized enough in relation to the experiences which I have had to undergo. I see that. Can my seeing it help me? A little, I think. Because I am more destructible than some other men, I must seek all the more to derive some advantage from what has a destructive effect on me, I must not take it as it is, but only in so far as it does service to my own truest life. Wherever I find such things, I must accept them in advance as indispensable material, without which my most inward being cannot ever entirely present itself. I must assimilate them, to arrange them eventually (as an artist, if I should wish to be one, and come to be one) as shadows to my light, to reproduce them as subordinate tones among which the tone of my soul springs out all the more livingly. What is pure can only be presented in terms of the impure, and if you try to give something of nobility without what is ordinary, then it will be most unnnatural and discordant, just because the noble thing itself, as it is expressed, wears the color of the destiny under which it originated, because the beautiful thing, as it presents itself in actuality, must needs assume, from among the conditions under which it arises, a form which is not natural to it, and which only becomes natural if one brings to it just those very conditions which of necessity gave it this form. The character of Brutus, for instance, is a most unnatural and incongruous one, if you do not see it in relation to the conditions which forced this *rigorous* form upon this *gentle* spirit. So, without the ordinary things, nothing noble can be presented; and I shall always tell myself, when in the world ordinary things strike upon me: You need them, just as the potter needs glaze, so accept them always, and do not reject them and do not be shy of them. That would be the answer. I wanted to ask your advice and thus precisely to describe my failings, of which you are naturally aware, to some extent, and also to bring them to my own mind; but I have got into deeper waters than I thought I would, and so that you may wholly understand my ponderings, I shall confess to you that my work has come to a standstill these last few days, which always makes me relapse into abstract reasoning. Perhaps my fugitive thoughts will make you reflect further on artists and art, especially, too, on my main failings as a poet, and on what can be done about them, and do please let me know what you think. . .

To HIS BROTHER[1]   *HOMBURG, JANUARY 1, 1799.*

[1] Karl Gock. He was Hölderlin's half-brother and six years younger.

I had put aside my usual work today and in my leisure have had all kinds of thoughts about the interest which the Germans now have in speculative philosophy, and in political literature as well, also, though to a less extent, in poetry. Perhaps you saw a short amusing article in the *Allgemeine Zeitung*, on the German Poets' Corps. It was this which set me thinking, and because you and I seldom philosophize nowadays, you will not think it a disservice if I write down my thoughts for you.

Reading in philosophy and politics do incontestibly have a good influence on the intellectual development of our nation, and perhaps the character of the German people, if I have been making a correct abstraction from my very imperfect experience, needed precisely that two-sided influence more than any other. I think, in fact, that the commonest virtues and failings of the Germans are to be reduced to their rather narrow domesticity. Everywhere they are *glebae addicti*,[1] and in some way most are, literally or figuratively, chained to their patch of soil, and, if it were to continue so, they would have in the end, like that good-hearted Dutch painter, to drag themselves to death with their own beloved—moral and physical—acquisitions and inheritance. Each is only at home in that to which he was born, and can seldom surmount its limits with his interests and ideas. Whence comes that lack of elasticity, of impulse, of a varied development of the faculties, whence comes the dark disdainful shyness, or also the fearful submissive blind worship, in regard to everything outside their timidly narrow sphere; whence, too, this insensibility to communal honor and communal property, which is of course very prevalent among modern peoples, but eminently so, I think, among the Germans. And just as only the man who lives in the open air is also happy in his room, so too is it impossible for individual life, to each his own, to persist without communal sense and open eyes for the world, and in fact among the Germans these two things have jointly declined, as it seems, and it does not speak very well for the apostles of restraint that among the Greeks, where each man belonged with mind and soul to the world around him, there is far more inner warmth to be found in single characters and

[1] Properly *glebae adscripsi* = bound to the soil (the term is legal, referring to land-tenure of serfs under feudal law).

situations than, for example, among us Germans, and the affected outcry of heartless cosmopolitanism and over-strenuous metaphysics can hardly be better shown up for what it is than by a noble pair like Thales and Solon, who walked through Greece and Asia and Egypt in order to acquaint themselves with the constitutional systems and the philosophers of the world, who were thus in more than one sense *generalized*, but at the same time very good friends, and more human and even more naive than all those together who try to persuade us not to open our eyes, not to open our hearts, to the world which is always worthy of it, lest the heart's naturalness should lose coherence.

. . .

Kant is the Moses of our nation, who leads them out of the Egyptian apathy into the free, lonely desert of his speculation, and who brings down the energetic law from the holy mountain. Of course, they still dance around their golden calf and hunger after their flesh-pots, and he would literally have had to make an exodus with them into some desert if they were to give up their belly-worship and their dead, heartless and senseless customs and opinions amid which their better living nature sighs inaudibly as in some deep dungeon . . . Moreover, the interest for philosophy and politics, if it were broader and more serious than it is, is by no means sufficient for the intellectual development of our nation, and it would be desirable that an end should be put to the boundless misunderstanding with which art, and especially poetry, is deprecated by the practitioners and appreciators of them. Much has already been said about the influence of the fine arts on the cultivation of the human mind, but it always turned out to seem no serious matter, and this was natural, for people did not consider what art is, and especially what poetry is, in their essential natures. They clung merely to poetry's unassuming exterior, which is of course inseparable from its essence, but is certainly not identical with it; they took it to be play, because it appears in the modest form of play, and so no effect other than play could reasonably be expected of it, play, that is, as distraction, almost the exact opposite of what poetry actually does when manifest in its true nature. For in poetry's presence, man immediately ingathers himself, and poetry gives him equanimity, not empty but living equanimity, in which all

18

the mind's faculties are alert, and are only not known in action because of the inmost harmony of poetry. Poetry brings men close, and it brings them together, not as play does—in which men are only joined in so far as each forgets himself and no one man's living singularity is brought to light.

. . . Poetry unites men, but not as play does; it unites them, in fact, if it is genuine and has a genuine effect, with all the various sorrows and joys and strivings and hopes and fears, with all their opinions and faults, all their virtues and ideas, with all great things and small things which exist among men, till they become a living thousand-membered inner whole, for it is precisely this that poetry itself should be, and the effect should match the cause. Do you not think, Karl, that the Germans could well use such a panacea, even when the political and philosophical cure is complete? For, when all is said and done, philosophical and political education does involve one inconvenience, namely that it may well bring men close to the essential and ineluctable conditions of life, with duty and justice, but how much is left over then for harmony in man? Foreground, center-ground and background, drawn in accord with the rules of optics, do not yet form by any means the landscape—which might perhaps stand beside the living work of nature. But the best Germans still think most often that everything would be all right if only the world were nice and *symmetrical*. O Greece, with your geniality and piety, where are you now? I too, with every good will, am simply groping in deed and thought after these unique people, and am only the more awkward and incongruous in what I do and say because I stand, like the geese, on flat feet in modern waters, and wing my way feebly toward the Greek heaven. Do not hold this figure against me. It is inept, but true, and between ourselves, I just wanted to say, it is not so bad.

. . .

To HIS MOTHER   *HOMBURG, JANUARY 1799.*

. . .

I agree with you completely, dearest mother, that it would do me good to obtain as assuming a position as possible, for indeed my perhaps unhappy inclination to poetry, which I have always withstood, with sincere effort, since my youth, by taking up so-called solider occupations, is still in me, and, as far as I can see from personal experience now, will remain in me as long as I live. I shall not judge whether it is imaginary, or a true impulse of my nature. But this much I do now know, that I have made myself profoundly restless and ill-humored, amongst other things, but directing my main attention and effort upon occupations which seem to suit my nature less well, e.g. philosophy, and this in all good faith, for I feared I might be called a mere poet. I was far from knowing why the study of philosophy, which ordinarily rewards with equanimity the tenacity which it demands, why it always made me, the less reservedly I surrendered to it, the more ill at ease, and even passionate; and now I find the explanation in my having deviated more than was necessary from my real inclination, and at such unnatural work my heart sighed for the occupation which it loved, as soldiering Swiss shepherds long for their valley and herd. Do not call this a sentimental longing. For why am I peaceful and good, like a child, when undisturbed in sweet leisure I practise this most innocent of occupations, which people only honor, of course, and rightly too, if it is done with mastery, a quality that my work perhaps may not yet have at all, because, ever since I was a boy, I never ventured to practise it as much as other things that I practised with perhaps a too good-natured conscientiousness, as a favor to my circumstances or to people's good will. And yet every art demands a whole human life, and the pupil must learn all things in their relation to his art if he is to develop his aptitude and not end by being suffocated.

. . .

To SUSETTE GONTARD   *HOMBURG, JUNE 1799.*
[*fragmentary draft*]

Every day I must summon back the vanished god. When I think of great men, in great epochs, how they, a holy fire, reached out around them and transformed everything dead, wooden, the straw of the world, into flame which flew with them into heaven, and then of myself, how I often walk around, a lamp flickering, and could beg for a drop of oil to let me shine through the night for a little longer, look, then through my body goes a strange trembling and softly to myself I speak the terrible words: living corpse.

Do you know why it is—men are afraid of each other, lest the genius of one consume the other, and so they allow themselves food and drink but nothing to nourish the soul, and they cannot endure it if something which they say and do, for once apprehended in the being of another, is transformed into flame. The fools! As if anything that men can say to each other were more than a kind of firewood, which only when it is seized by the intellectual fire becomes fire once more, just as it came from life and fire. And if they only give each other nourishment, then they live and shine, both of them, and neither consumes the other.

Do you remember our quiet times together, when we and we alone surrounded each other? That was a triumph. We two, so free and proud and wide-awake and flowering and splendid in soul and heart and eye and face, and beside each other in such heavenly peace! I suspected it then, and said it: one might well walk all through the world and hardly find things the same again. And every day I feel this more seriously.

To NEUFFER   *HOMBURG, JULY3, 1799.*

I'll take this chance to tell you—if it should interest you—a little about the method and means by which I wrote 'Emilie'.[1] You can imagine that haste prevented me from writing in the way which I had long planned, as I would like to have done, and as would have been necessary in order to make perceptible what are probably the good points in the plan, especially as regards subjects that are not properly heroic. My concern is not at all with the externals of novelty; but I feel and see more and more how we are vacillating between the two extremes: that of licence, and that of blind subservience to old forms which constrain us and which we misapply. Do not think, dear friend, that I am thus capriciously thinking up for myself a form that is all my own; I examine my feeling, as it leads me to this or that, and of course I ask myself whether or not a form which I choose contradicts the central idea, and especially, too, the

[1] One of the poems of the Homburg period, an idyl, intended for a miscellany published by Steinkopf of Stuttgart. The letter illustrates aspects of the poetics which Hölderlin was working out in Homburg.

21

subject which the form treats. Naturally, I can be right in a general sense, but in the actual writing I can make false moves all the more easily, because I follow only myself and can adhere to no existing model. But there is simply no choice; the moment we take a subject which is the least bit modern, we have, I am certain, to abandon the old classical forms which are so intrinsically molded to their subjects that they are useless for others. Of course, for us it is quite usual if a love story, for instance, which is *no more than just that,* appears in the form of a tragedy; but the tragic form's inner trend and its heroic dialogue, as treated by classical authors, does not suit a love story at all. If you keep the heroic dialogue, it is always as if the lovers were having a quarrel. If you abandon it, the tone contradicts the proper form of the tragedy, which then need not be strictly preserved, of course, but in our times has lost for this reason its proper poetic value and meaning. Moreover, people only want stirring and exciting moments and situations; writer and public seldom trouble about the meaning and impression of the whole. Thus the most rigorous of all poetic forms, whose entire function is to move forward, naked and unadorned, in harmonious modulations, almost entirely in pure major tones, each of which is itself a self-contained whole, and which in this proud rejection of all accidentals presents the central idea of a living whole, with maximum conciseness, completeness and substantial meaning, and thus with more clarity and gravity than all other known poetic forms—the tragic form in its dignity has been debased into an opportunistic means of saying something brilliant or tender. But then what else could be done with it, short of choosing the subject to which it was suited, and in conjunction with which alone it would acquire meaning and vitality. It could only die, like all other forms, once they lose the living soul for which they served as organic physical structures, and out of which they took their origin and shape—just as, for instance, the republican form in our cities has become dead and meaningless because men are not fit to *need* it, to say the least.

Now as tragic subjects are made to move forward in pure major *autonomous* tones, harmoniously modulating, and to present a whole that is charged with energetic and meaningful parts, with a minimum of accidentals, so are sentimental

22

subjects, love for instance, entirely suited for moving forward in harmonious modulations not in major tones, proud and firm, and not with a decisive rejection of accidentals, but with this *delicate diffidence toward accidentals*, and in deep, full tones whose meaning is elegiac, tones which are highly evocative, because of the longing and the hope which they express, and for presenting the central idea of a living whole not by means of this tensed energy of parts and this sweeping movement forward, not with this quick brevity, but winged, like Psyche and Eros, and with *intimate* brevity, and now it only remains to be seen in what form this can be achieved with the most ease, naturalness and authenticity, so that love's beautiful spirit can acquire its own poetic structure and mode.

Forgive me if I weary you with this vague reasoning. I live so much in solitude that it is pleasant for me, when I have an hour's leisure, to converse in writing with an open-minded friend, about things which are on my mind, and this makes me, as you see, more loquacious than is agreeable to the other person. And as a matter of fact I have said as good as nothing, and have been talking more to myself than to you.

I am delighted that you are giving more and more of your time to poetry. The epoch has flung upon us such a load of impressions that—and this feeling grows on me day by day —only by prolonged work, reaching into old age, and by earnest effort, starting afresh over and over again, shall we be able to produce in the end that to which we have been primarily destined by nature and which perhaps under other conditions might have ripened earlier but hardly to such perfection . . .

To SUSETTE GONTARD   *HOMBURG, NOVEMBER 1799.*
[*fragmentary draft*]

It is worth all the tears we have wept these years, for being unable to possess the joy that we can give each other, but terrible for us to think that because we lack each other we both perhaps must perish with the best that is in us. And look, it is this which sometimes silences me, because I must stop myself thinking such thoughts. Your illness, your letter —again I saw, however much I may become unseeing in other ways, that you are always, always suffering, —and, boy that I am, all I can do is weep. —Tell me, is it better to say or not to say what is in our hearts? I have always played the coward, to spare you, —have always behaved as if I could acquiesce in everything, as if I were made just as a plaything of people and circumstance, and had no steadfast heart in me which would fight loyally and freely in its own right for what it loves best, my dearest life, have often renounced and denied my dearest love, even my thoughts of you sometimes, simply in order to bear, for your sake, this destiny as gently as I can, —you too, my peaceful one, have always struggled for equanimity, have endured heroically, and have been silent about what cannot be changed, have within you hidden and buried your heart's eternal choice, and this is why there is often a twilight around us, and we no longer know what we are and what we have, and hardly know ourselves any more; this eternal struggle and contradiction in your mind, it must slowly kill you, and, if no God can calm it there, then I have no choice but to pine away because of you and me, or to ignore everything but you and seek with you a way to end the struggle.

I have thought that we might live on renunciation, that this perhaps might make us strong enough to say, for all time goodbye to hope,

The fragment ends with the comma. This and the previous letter to Susette Gontard exist only as fragments. It is believed that they were never sent to her, for fear of upsetting her; but it is not certain. She died of smallpox on June 22, 1802, at the age of thirty-three.

To CHRISTIAN GOTTFRIED SCHÜTZ
HOMBURG, WINTER 1799–1800.

. . .

A close study of the Greeks has helped me and served me, in lieu of discussion with friends, in the solitude of my thoughts, not to become too assured or too uncertain. Also the results of my studies differ from those of others I know. As you realize, people have often quite misunderstood the rigor with which the great classical authors distinguished between their various forms of poetry, or have only touched on externals, judging the art of the Greeks to be much more a well-calculated amusement, than a holy decorum needed for the treatment of divine things. To the Greeks, the su-

24

premely intellectual must have been also the supremely characteristic.[1] Thus, too, the presentation of the supremely intellectual. Thence the rigor and sharpness of form in their literature, thence the noble violence with which, in subordinate forms of poetry, they observed this rigor, thence the delicate tact with which in the higher forms of poetry they avoided the salient characteristic, precisely because the supremely characteristic contains nothing alien or inessential to itself and therefore no trace of constraint. Thus they presented the divine humanly, but avoiding always the actual human scale, in a natural manner, because poetry, being in its whole essence, its enthusiasm,[2] as in its modesty and restraint, a serene worship of the god, may never make gods into men or men into gods, never practise impure idolatry, but may only bring gods and men closer to one another. Tragedy shows this *per contrarium*. God and man seem to be one, and to be one destiny, which excites all the humility and pride of man, and finally leaves behind on the one hand an awe of what is of heaven, and on the other hand a purified sensibility as man's property . . .

To HIS SISTER
   HAUPTWYL [SWITZERLAND], FEBRUARY 23, 1801[3]

I am writing to you and our dear family on the day when for us here everything is full of the news of the peace treaty,[4] and, because you know me, I do not need to tell you how this makes me feel. Even this morning, when the master of the house greeted me with the news, there was little I could

---

[1] In what follows, Hölderlin's argument hinges on his use of the term "das Charakteristische", a technical term in 18th century esthetics. He aligns his categories of "supremely intellectual" (*das Geistigste,* which connotes "divine intelligence") and the "supremely characteristic" (*das Höchstcharakteristiche*), as if the Greeks viewed the "divine" itself as being the latter. These categories are then distinguished from the "salient characteristic" (*das Hauptcharakteristische*) which is closer to the actual and concrete.

[2] *Enthusiasmus* in the original, with the root sense of "in the god".

[3] Hölderlin had gone to Hauptwyl as a private tutor.

[4] The Peace of Lunéville, 9 February 1801.

25

say. But the bright blue of the sky and the clear sun over the nearby Alps were at that moment all the more dear in my sight, because otherwise I would not have known where to turn my eyes for joy.

. . .

This and the greatness of nature in these regions wonderfully elevate and calm my mind. You would stand as amazed as I do before these shining eternal mountains, and if the god of power has a throne on earth, then it is upon these glorious peaks.

I can only stand there, like a child, and marvel and quietly rejoice, whenever I am outside, on the nearest hill, and when out of the ether all the slopes descend,[1] closer and closer, into this friendly valley whose sides are garlanded with evergreen fir forests, and where, deep down, streams and lakes pour through, and there I live, in a garden, where at my feet stand willow and poplar, beside a clear river which at night delights me with its murmuring, when everything is quiet and I write and ponder with the serene starlit sky before me.

You see, my dear, I view my stay here as a man who has suffered enough in his youth and is now satisfied and undisturbed enough to give thanks from his heart for that which is. And the more inwardly tranquil my mind becomes, the brighter and livelier in me is my remembrance of you . . .

To CASIMIR ULRICH BOHLENDORFF
NÜRTINGEN, DECEMBER 4, 1801.

. . .

Your work now has much more precision and skilled suppleness and has lost none of its warmth; on the contrary, the elasticity of your mind has, like a good blade, been made more strong by schooling in flexion.[2] I wish you good luck in this especially. Nothing is harder for us to learn than the free use of what is native to us. And I think that clarity of representation is to us originally as natural as the fire from

[1] *Aether* in Hölderlin's poems is the supreme aerial substance of life in which the divine dwells.

[2] Literally "in the bending school" *(in der beugenden Schule).* Böhlendorff had sent Hölderlin an advance copy of his play, *Fernando oder die Kunstweihe,* 1802.

heaven was to the Greeks.[1] Precisely for this reason, they can be *surpassed* in comely passion, which you sustain, rather than in that Homeric presence of mind and gift for representing things.

It sounds paradoxical. But I say it again and offer it for your reflection and use: a peculiarly native quality becomes less salient as the cultivation of the mind proceeds. Therefore the Greeks are in less degree masters of holy pathos, because it was innate in them, whereas they excel, on the other hand, in the gift for representing things, from Homer onward, because this extraordinary man had the profundity and greatness of soul to acquire for his Apollonian realm the occidental *Junonian restraint*, and thus truly to make the alien his own.

With us the opposite is the case. Therefore, too, it is so dangerous to abstract our rules for art exclusively from Greek excellence. I have labored for a long time on this question, and now I know that, discounting what must be the supreme thing for the Greeks and for ourselves, namely living proportion and skill, there is nothing in which we can *equal* them.

But what is proper to oneself must be as well learned as what is alien. Therefore the Greeks are indispensable to us. It is simply that we shall not approach them in that which is proper and native to us, because, as I have said, the most difficult thing is the *free* use of what is proper to oneself.

. . .

Of myself, and how I have been getting on till now, how far I have remained and become worthy of you and my friends, also what I am doing and shall produce, however little it is, I shall soon tell you when I write from the vicinity of your Spain, that is, from Bordeaux, for which I shall be leaving next week as private tutor and chaplain in a German evangelical household.[2] I shall have to keep my wits about me pretty well, in France, in Paris; I am also looking forward to seeing the sea, and the sun of Provence.

[1] "The fire from heaven" *(das Feuer vom Himmel)* = the Apollonian "holy pathos" (see next paragraph). Hölderlin's views in some ways reverse those current at the time, anticipating Nietzsche by 70 years.

[2] There was some misunderstanding which made Hölderlin think that he would have to act as a chaplain.

My friend, the world that lies before me is brighter than usual, and more serious. Yes, I like it the way things are, as when in summer the "ancient holy father shakes from reddish cloud with an easy hand his benign lightning."[1] For among all the things that I see of God, this sign has become my special elected one. Once I could rejoice over a new truth, a better view of what is above and around us, but now I have my fears that I shall end like Tantalus, who had from the gods more than his fill.

But I do what I can, as best I can, and, whenever I see that my way is leading me where it led the others, I think that it is a godless and mad thing to seek a way which is assured against attack; and that no grass grows for death alone.

Well, goodbye for the present, my dear friend. I am full of departure now. It is a long time since I wept. But it cost me bitter tears to decide to leave my homeland now, perhaps for ever. For what do I love more in all the world? But they have no use for me. I shall remain German, and must, of course, even if the needs of my heart and the need to make a living were to drive me to Tahiti . . .

To HIS MOTHER   *BORDEAUX, JANUARY 28, 1802.*

At last, my dear mother, I am here, am well looked after, am well, and certainly mean not to forget the gratitude which I owe to the lord of life and death. I cannot write much at present; I arrived this morning, and my mind is too much taken up with my new situation for me to tell you with equanimity things of interest about the journey now past. Moreover, so much has happened to me that I can hardly speak of it.

These last days I walked through a single beautiful Spring, but just before that, on the terrifying snow-covered heights of the Auvergne, in storm and wilderness, in the icy night and with loaded pistols by me in my rough bed—it was then, too, that I said a prayer which was the best I ever prayed till now, and which I shall not forget.

I am safe—give thanks with me.

[1] Hölderlin quotes freely here from Goethe's poem "Grenzen der Menschheit". Goethe has "from rolling clouds" and the "age-old father" and "sows over the earth".

My dears, when I had come through the dangers, I greeted you in thought, as if I were newborn—at once I reproached myself for not having named in particular our dear grandmother when I last wrote from Lyons, I spoke with you, dear mother, saw my sister's image, and wrote in my glad thoughts a letter to my Karl in lofty tones.

I am steeled and dedicated now, through and through, as you would wish me to be. I think that I shall remain so, for the most part. To fear nothing and take much as it comes. How good it will be for me—sure refreshing sleep. I am living almost too grandly. I would be glad of sure simplicity ...

It was probably in Bordeaux, if not on the journey there, that Hölderlin began to go mad. It is believed that he made the greater part of the journey from Lyons to Bordeaux on foot (about 600 km). From Lyons he probably took the present Route Nationale 89, through Clermont, along the northern heights of the Monts d'Auvergne, to Périgueux. From here he would have walked through the Périgueux valley, which, being open to warm south-east winds from the Atlantic, would have made a "single beautiful Spring" possible even in January (see Adolf Beck's commentary, "Grosse Stuttgarter Ausgabe", 6,2, pp. 1083–4). He left Bordeaux—under what circumstances it is not known—soon after May 10, and tramped home via the Vendée, possibly Paris, then Stuttgart, arriving in mid-June at his mother's house in Nürtingen. The Vendée region (the coast-line south of the Loire delta) had been the scene of bloody fighting between royalist inhabitants and republican troops during the years 1793–96. Hence the detail in the next letter.

To CASIMIR ULRICH BOHLENDORFF
NÜRTINGEN, NOVEMBER 1802.

It is long since I wrote; meanwhile I have been in France and have seen the sad, lonely earth; the shepherds of southern France and things of beauty here and there, men and women who have grown up in fear of divided loyalty and of hunger.

The mighty element, the fire from heaven and the tranquility of men, their life in nature, and their confinedness and content, absorbed me continually, and I can well say, as is said of heroes, that Apollo has struck me.

The ferocity and warlikeness of the regime bordering on the Vendée interested me, the purely male, which has the

29

very light of life in eye and limb, and which, in the feel of death, feels a kind of virtuosity and quenches its thirst for knowledge.

The athletic character of southern people, in the ruins of the ancient spirit, made me more familiar with the true essence of the Greeks; I understand their nature and wisdom, their body, how they grew in their climate, and the rules they observed to shield their exuberant genius from the elemental power.

This determined their popular character,[1] their way of accepting and communicating with alien natures, from this they took their singular invduality, which shows forth vitally in so far as supreme understanding is, to the Greek, the power to reflect the actual, and we comprehend this once we comprehend the heroic body of the Greeks; their popular character is sensitive receptivity, as ours is [restraint].[2]

Ancient statues impressed me in a way which gave me better to understand not only the Greeks but altogether the supreme thing in art, which, even in the most intense movement and phenomenalization of ideas and of all serious meaning still conserves all things in their status and independence, so that accordingly assuredness is the supreme kind of sign.

After several shocks and disturbances to my mind, I had to settle down, for a time, and meanwhile I have been staying in my home town.

Nature here at home absorbs me more strongly, the more I study it. Storm, not only in its full power, but precisely as a power and a shape, among the other heavenly forms, light

[1] The translation of *Popularität* as "popular character" [native, indigenous character] follows A. Beck (*Grosse Stuttgarter Ausgabe,* 6,2, p. 1089). But nowhere else among Hölderlin's various terms denoting the general mentality of a people, Greek or German, does this word appear. Fichte, in a letter dated June 27, 1795, to Schiller, uses the word to mean the "public appeal" of a literary work. Hölderlin could have heard Fichte use the word this way; he might have intended, in this letter, something like "public stance" in the sense of "open-mindedness".

[2] Scholars argue that Hölderlin accidentally omitted a word here. Most agree that *Nüchternheit,* translated here as "restraint", would complete the meaning intended.

in its operations, shaping forms, natively and as a principle and mode of destiny, so that something should be holy for us, its pressure as it comes and goes, the characteristic forests and the congruence, in a single region, of different natural characters, bringing all the holy places of earth together in one place, and the philosophical light around my window, is now my joy; may I keep in mind how I came thus far!

My dear friend, I think that we shall not echo the poets down to our time, but our song will take on a quite different character, and that we are not appreciated because we, after the Greeks, are beginning once more to sing indigenously and naturally, with proper originality.

But write soon. I need your clear tones. Psyche among friends, and growth of thought in conversation and letter is needed by artists. Otherwise we have no thought for ourself; but it belongs to the holy image which we are shaping. Farewell.

This letter to Böhlendorff is almost alone among those dated 1802–06, written between sanity and insanity, to give a glimpse into the imagination of the poet during the period of the last visionary hymns. In September 1806, Hölderlin was taken to the Authenrieth clinic at Tübingen. About a year later he was taken, harmless and incurable, into the personal care of a Tübingen carpenter named Zimmer, in whose house he lived until his death in 1843.

The letters of
RIMB D

Rimbaud's earliest extant letter was written in 1870, when Rimbaud was fifteen and a half years old, though he says in the letter that he is seventeen. The ms of this letter shows that Rimbaud had first written presque, *or* almost, *seventeen, then marked out the* almost. *He wrote from Charleville, his native town near the Belgian border, where he had shown a precocious talent for composing verse at the local collège or high school. The already well known poet, Théodore de Banville, to whom Rimbaud addressed his letter, was a member of the so-called Parnassian group in Paris, that had begun to publish a monthly collection of verse entitled* Le Parnasse Contemporain. *Banville was one of the editors of this collection, which to the adolescent Rimbaud, a schoolboy in the provinces, represented the height of poetic renown at that time. Rimbaud enclosed three of his earliest poems in this letter—"Sensation", "Ophélie", "Credo in unam" (lated titled "Soleil et Chair"). They were not taken by Banville, though he replied kindly to the boy.*

To THÉODORE DE BANVILLE

CHARLEVILLE, 24 MAY 1870.

Dear Master,

We are in the months of love; I am seventeen. The age of hopes and chimeras, as they say, —and here I have begun, child touched by the finger of the Muse, —pardon if that's banal—to tell my fine beliefs, my hopes, my sensations, all these affairs of the poets, —I call that, spring.

If I send you a few of these verses, —by way of Alphonse Lemerre, the excellent publisher, —it is because I love all the poets, all the good Parnassians, —since the poet is a Parnassian, —seized by ideal beauty; it is because I love in you, very simply, a descendant of Ronsard, a brother of our masters of 1830, a true romantic, a true poet. That is why. —it's foolish, isn't it? but still . . .

In two years, in one year perhaps, I will be in Paris.

I too, gentlemen of the Press,[1] I will be a Parnassian!

I do not know what I have there[2] that wants to rise up. I swear, dear Master, always to worship two goddesses, the Muse and Liberty.

[1] In the 19th century, newspapers played a much larger part in the printing of poetry than they do today. Rimbaud's principal source of information about poets and poetry in Paris was from Parisian newspapers that he read in Charleville, at least at the beginning of his career.

[2] Rimbaud means inside himself.

34

Don't frown too much while reading these verses: You would make me crazy with joy and hope, if you would, dear Master, manage to make a little room for the poem *Credo in unam* among the Parnassians. I would appear in the latest number of *Parnasse*: it would become the Credo of the poets! —Ambition! oh madness!

(At this point in his letter Ribaud wrote out the three poems he was submitting to Banville.)

If these verses found a place in *Parnasse contemporain*? Are they not the faith of poets?

I am unknown; what does it matter? poets are brothers. These verses believe; they love; they hope: that is all.

Dear Master, mine: Lift me up a little: I am young; hold out your hand to me—

Rimbaud's first mentor was a young teacher, Georges Izambard, who had come to the College in Charleville in January of 1870. Izambard encouraged Rimbaud in the writing of poetry, and when he left Charleville for the summer, after the end of the school year, he gave Rimbaud access to his apartment where the boy could read in Izambard's library, containing a selection of contemporary literature, especially poetry, since Izambard had some ambition to be a poet himself. Not very long afterward, Rimbaud felt his teacher's inadequacies and the enthusiasm of his initial devotion to the man vanished, to be replaced by indifference, even contempt. In any case, what Rimbaud really wished was to make contact with the literary world of Paris, as this letter makes clear, and this world was made even more unavailable to him than before by the outbreak of the Franco-Prussian War in the summer of 1870, which drastically cut communication between Charleville and the capital. Izambard was staying in the town of Douai at this time.

To GEORGE IZAMBARD *CHARLEVILLE, 25 AUGUST 1870.*

You, you are lucky not to be living any longer in Charleville.

My native town is superlatively idiotic among little provincial towns. About that, be sure, I have no more illusions. Because it is near Mezières[1]—a town one doesn't visit—be-

---

[1] Mezières was a garrison town not far from Charleville. Rimbaud's father, a Captain of Infantry, had been stationed there when he met Rimbaud's mother, the daughter of local

cause it sees two or three hundred soldiers in red trousers pass through its streets, this blessed population gesticulates, pompously bravoes, very different from the besieged at Metz and at Strasburg! It's terrific, the retired grocers who put on the uniform! It's amazing how courageous they behave, lawyers, glaziers, tax-collectors, carpenters, all the big stomachs, who, rifles at ready, go on patrols at the gates of Mezières; my country rises! Me, I prefer to watch it from my seat; don't move your boots! That's my principle.

I am out of my element, sick, furious, stupid, turned upside down; I was hoping for sunbaths, endless walks, repose, journeys, adventures, a gypsy life, in short; I was hoping, above all, for newspapers, for books—Nothing! Nothing! The mail no longer brings anything to the bookstores; Paris ignores us nicely: not a single new book! it's death! Here I am reduced, in the matter of newspapers, to the respectable *Courrier des Ardennes*—publisher, editor, manager, chief reporter and only reporter: A. Pouillard! This newspaper sums up the aspirations, the prayers, and the opinions of the population: so imagine! what a dirty trick! One is exiled in one's own country!!

Luckily, I have your room: —you remember you gave me permission. I have carried off half your books! .... I've read all your books, all; three days ago I got down to *Les Epreuves*, then to *Les Glaneuses*—yes, I reread that book![1] —then that was all! Nothing more; your library, my last plank of salvation, was exhausted! *Don Quixote* appeared before me; yesterday I spent two hours looking over Doré's woodcuts: now, I have nothing more!

I send you some verses; read them one morning, in the sunlight, as I wrote them: you are not a professor any more now, I hope!

(There is a missing portion of the letter at this point. Rimbaud

land owners and farmers. After six years of marriage he left his wife and family; Rimbaud never saw him again.

[1] *Les Glaneuses* was a first volume of poems by Paul Demény, a friend of Izambard's, and also a teacher. Rimbaud would later meet him at Douai and address several of his most important letters to him. Demény published another volume of verse but is now known only because of his connection with Rimbaud.

It is as beautiful as the laments of Antigone in Sophocles.

I have the *Fêtes Galantes* of Paul Verlaine. It is very bizarre, very curious; but truly charming. At times great poetic licenses: for example,

Et la tigresse épou—vantable d'Hycranie is one verse in this volume.

Buy, I advise you, *La Bonne Chanson*, a little book of verse by the same poet: it has just appeared, published by Lemerre; I haven't read it: nothing comes here; but several newspapers speak very well of it.

Goodbye, send me a letter of 25 pages—general delivery—and very quickly!

A. Rimbaud

P.S. Soon some revelations on the life I'm going to lead after the vacations.

Shortly after writing this letter to Izambard, Rimbaud makes the first of several trips to Paris, equipped with insufficient money and virtually no knowledge of how to survive in a large city. He has to be rescued by his mother and Izambard, who have him sent back to Douai and to Charleville. He is in Paris during the siege by the Prussian Army, shortly before the Commune, returning home on foot through the Prussian lines. During this year he composes a number of poems, and his famous Lettres du Voyant, the first addressed to Izambard, the the second, longer one to Demény, the only poet of any sort whom he knew personally at this time. These two letters are now easily available in a number of translations and for this reason are not repeated here. Rimbaud wrote somewhat later to Demény asking him for advice about how to get a job in Paris, so that he could manage to live there permanently, after his unsuccessful, temporary visits. It appears that Demény had replaced Izambard in Rimbaud's confidence, though Demény was to prove of little help and soon dropped from Rimbaud's life altogether.

Sir,

You make me state my request again: so be it. Here is the whole lament. I'm searching for calm words: but my skill in the art is not very profound. Well, here it is.

Situation of the prisoner: For more than a year I have given up ordinary life for what you know. Shut up without respite in this unspeakable Ardennais country, keeping company with no one, absorbed in a disreputable occupation,[1] inept, obstinate, mysterious, replying only with silence to questions, to rude and spiteful reprimands, asserting my dignity in my extra-special position, I have finally provoked some odious resolutions in a mother as inflexible as seventy-three managing directors with vizors of lead.

She wanted to sentence me to labor, —for life, in Charleville (Ardennes)! A job on such and such a day, she said, or out the door. —I refused this kind of life, without giving my reasons: that would have been contemptible. Up till to-day, I've been able to get round these expiration dates. She has come to this: to wish unceasingly for me to run away, escape! Destitute, inexperienced, I would end up in a reformatory. And, from that moment, nothing more would be heard of me!

There's the disgusting handkerchief that's been stuffed in my mouth. It's very simple.

I ask for nothing, I ask for information. I want to work independently: but in Paris which I love. Look: I am a man on foot, nothing more; I arrive in the huge city with no material resource: but you have told me: Someone who wants to be a laborer at fifteen sous a day applies at such and such a place, does such and such, lives in a certain way. I apply, I do it, I live like that. I have asked you to name some jobs that would take little thought, for thought demands large amounts of time. Leaving the poet free, these dull see-saws become pleasing. I am in Paris: I must live with absolute *economy*! Don't you find that sincere? As for me, it seems to me so strange, that I must protest my seriousness to you!

I had had the above idea: the only one which appeared reasonable to me: I express it for you in different words. I have good will, I do what I can, I speak as intelligibly as an

---

[1] Writing poetry.

unhappy man may! Why scold the child who, not endowed with the rudiments of zoology, would wish for a bird with five wings? One would only make him change his faith to birds with six tails, or with three beaks! What one should do is lend him a Buffon of the bird families: that would undelude him.

So, not knowing what you will be able to write me, I cut short my explanations and continue to trust in your experience, in your obligingness which I certainly blessed, on receiving your letter, and I urge you a little to proceed with my ideas, —please.

Would you without too much annoyance receive some examples of my work?

When Demény evidently failed to be of help, a man named Charles Bretagne, a local customs-official with an interest in literature and with rather eccentric ways, whom Rimbaud had met in a café in Charleville, encouraged him to write to Paul Verlaine, the most famous of the younger poets in Paris and already a great enthusiasm of Rimbaud's from a distance. In his initial letter to Verlaine (which is lost) Rimbaud enclosed four of his recent poems, and when Verlaine did not answer immediately—he was absent from Paris at the time—Rimbaud sent off a second letter (also lost) containing additional poems. In his impatience and anxiety to win Verlaine's approval, Rimbaud posted a third letter, the one included here. Only a portion of it has been preserved.

To PAUL VERLAINE   *CHARLEVILLE, SEPTEMBER 1871.*

I have made plans to compose an ambitious poem, and I cannot work at Charleville. I am prevented from coming to Paris, being without resources. My mother is a widow and extremely pious. She gives me only ten centimes every Sunday to pay for my chair at church.

Verlaine's famous reply, at last, to Rimbaud is well known. "Venez, chère grande âme, on vous appelle, on vous attend." (Come, dear and great soul, we call you, we await you.) The story of Verlaine's and Rimbaud's year together in Paris is also sufficiently famous not to need repetition here. By April of 1872 Rimbaud was back in Charleville, in a bitter mood, and reproaching Verlaine for not managing to keep him in Paris. Only fragments of this letter survive.

To PAUL VERLAINE   *CHARLEVILLE, APRIL 1872.*

When you will see me actually eating excrement, only then will you no longer find that I cost too much to feed! . . .

Soon in Paris again, where Verlaine had got him a room, Rimbaud writes to a school friend from his days at the Collège in Charleville, Ernest Delahaye. He and Delahaye had shared certain radical political views and youthful romantic effusions and cynicisms, and though Delahaye developed none of Rimbaud's talent, he apparently represented to Rimbaud a trustworthy and sympathetic friend. Rimbaud addressed a number of his best letters to Delahaye during the next three or four years and corresponded with him off and on until the end of his life.

To ERNEST DELAHAYE   *PARIS, JUNE 1872.*[1]

Yes, existence is extraordinary in the Ardennes cosmorama. The province, where one is nurtured on flour-meal and mud, where one drinks the local wine and beer, that's not what I miss. So you are right to denounce it unremittingly. But this place here: distilling, mixing, everything jammed together; and the suffocating summer: the heat is not continuous, but seeing that warm weather is to everyone's advantage, and that everyone's a pig, I hate summer, which kills me when it makes itself felt a little.[2] I feel a thirst, and

[1] Actually, Rimbaud dated this letter, "Parmerde, Jumphe 1872." He and Verlaine had begun to use an argot, sometimes obscene, sometimes merely fanciful, in their letters and some of their poems, especially Rimbaud's. The argot tradition is, of course, very old in French poetry, going back to Villon, with whom Rimbaud identified himself. "Parmerde" hardly requires explanation; "Jumphe" may be a play on the rather pretentious renaming of the months of the year during the French Revolution. The Revolutionary Calendar was drawn up by the poet Fabre D'Eglantine. Rimbaud would seem to be making his own version here, thinking of himself as a revolutionary poet, too. He had been enthusiastic over the Commune and the collapse of the Second Empire. Delahaye would catch the allusion behind "Jumphe" since he and Rimbaud agreed politically. Yet the word seems more playful than serious.

[2] Five years later he would say to Delahaye, "Je ne puis plus vivre que dans les pays chauds" (I can't live any more except

40

danger of gangrene: the rivers of the Ardennes, the caves, that is what I miss.

Fortunately there is a bar here that I like better. Long live the Academy of Absinthe, in spite of the ill will of the waiters! It is the most exquisite and tingling of habits, intoxication by virtue of this glacial herb, absinthe! Except, afterwards, lying down in filth!

Always the same complaint, no! What is certain, is: *merde* on Perrin.[1] And on the counter of the Univers[2] whether it faces the square or not. I don't curse the Universe, however. . . But all that is the usual stuff.

What is serious is that you should torment yourself so. Perhaps it would be good sense for you to walk a lot and read. Good sense in any case not to confine yourself in offices and parental houses. Debauches should take place away from such spots. I am far from selling balm, but I believe that bad habits do not offer consolations, to our pitiful days.

Now it's at night that I work. From midnight until five in the morning. Last month my room, on rue Monsieur-le-Prince, looked on a garden of the lycée Saint Louis. There were enormous trees under my narrow window. At three o'clock in the morning the candle paled: all the birds cried at once in the trees. Finished. No more work. I had to look at the trees, the sky, seized by this indescribable hour, the first of the morning. I saw the dormitories, absolutely deaf. And already the sound, lumbering, sonorous, delicious, of the carts on the boulevards. I smoked my hammer-headed

in hot countries), and there are the lines from *Une Saison en Enfer:* "Je reviendrai, avec des membres de fer, la peau sombre . . . Les femmes soignent ces féroces infirmes retour des pays chauds." Rimbaud lived the latter part of his life in Abyssinia.

[1] Henri Perrin took Izambard's place as professor of rhetoric at the Collège. Subsequently he became editor of a newspaper, *Le Nord-Est,* printed in Charleville. Rimbaud submitted a couple of poems to him, which he rejected. Perrin disliked Rimbaud and gave orders to the concierge in the building where he lived to refuse admittance to the "young man with long hair."

[2] The Univers was the name of a cafe in Charleville, where Rimbaud had hung out and where his bad manners had made him unwelcome. There is a possible play here on the word— Rimbaud telling Delahaye his dislike does not extend to the universe in general, the second time he uses the word.

pipe, spitting on the tiles, for it was a mansard roof, my room. At five o'clock, I would go down to buy some bread. This is the hour. The workers are on their way everywhere. It's the time to get drunk at the wine sellers, for me. I would come back home to eat, and go to bed at seven in the morning, when the sun brought the woodlice out from under the tiles. The first morning of summer, and the evenings in December, that is what has always thrilled me here.

But, at the moment, I have a lovely room, on a bottomless courtyard, but ten feet square.—Rue Victor Cousin makes a corner at the Place de la Sorbonne by the Café du Bas-Rhin and leads into the run Soufflot, at the other end.—There (in my room), I drink water all night, I don't see the morning come, I don't sleep, I suffocate. And that's life.

It will most certainly be made right at your request![1] Don't forget to defecate on *La Renaissance,* a literary and artistic magazine, if you meet it. I've avoided up till now plagues of slimy emigrants.[2] And merde on the seasons and furious rage.[3]

Courage.

Rimbaud's career as a poet was extremely brief, as is well known, probably not more than four years. His correspondence during this time when he can be thought of as a poet is quite limited, principally because Verlaine's wife, who was ashamed and angered at the liaison between Rimbaud and her husband, destroyed letters written by Rimbaud to Verlaine. Rimbaud spent the last seventeen or eighteen years of his life trying to make money, ultimately as a trader in Arabia and Abyssinia. Rimbaud died at Marseilles in November, 1891, at the age of thirty-seven, probably from a widespread cancer that began in his right knee. Supposedly he received the final rites of the Catholic Church immediately before his death. The last words we actually have of his, however, are from a letter dated the day before death; these words are, among others, "à bord," "à bord," meaning a ship to Suez, (it would have been necessary to carry him on board).

[1] Rimbaud is being ironic in respect to his lot in life, in particular his disagreeable room, and to his life in general, which will "most certaintly" or most probably not be made right at his request. He is using the language of hotel proprietors and businesses who promise to satisfy the customer. This sort of

commercial language appears in the prose poems *Les Illumina-tions* which he was probably writing at this time. It is one facet of his multiple tone.

[2] Rimbaud's French is, "pestes d'émigrés caropolmerdis," a phrase that pretty well defies translation. Perhaps a Joyce could cope with "caropolmerdis", and in fact, rather than argot, it appears to be more a portmanteau word, as do other expressions of Rimbaud's, such as "rendez-vol" instead of rendezvous, Rimbaud's term being much more charged with meaning than the usual word, into which it should not be translated back, as critics have usually done. The nearest approach to "caropolmerdis" might be something like the Host's curse on the Pardoner at the end of Chaucer's "The Pardoner's Tale"—"I wolde I hadde thy coillons in myn hond/In stide of relikes or of sein-tuarie./Lat kutte hem of, I wol thee helpe hem carie;/They shul be shryned in an hogges toord!" Rimbaud's phrase, coming as it does just after a scathing reference to a new literary maga-zine, is perhaps his way of describing effete, fishy, or sticky artistic types in Paris, whom he was avoiding. Rimbaud's manners were often quite purposely tough, even coarse, and he made enemies of practically all the other writers he came in contact with at Paris.

[3] Rimbaud's spelling here is "colrage", which has usually been corrected to "courage", since Verlaine and Rimbaud had a habit of changing their -ou's to -ol's. Also it appears that Rim-baud wanted Delahaye to understand he meant courage by repeating the word in its normal spelling. So, editors have made it a kind of double courage, as it were. However, when one considers the phrase in which the first "colrage" appears—"Et merde aux saisons et colrage"—it strikes one that Rimbaud may well have meant the word exactly as he wrote it; that is to say, as a combination of *colère* and *rage*. The second, normally spelled "courage", separated as a final parting note all to itself, would then modulate and deepen his attitude in the direction of saner judgment, always a tendency in Rimbaud, that runs counter to his enfant terrible reputation. Witness a line of this letter to Delahaye—"mais je crois que les habitudes n'offrent pas des consolations. . . ." However, in the end it must be taken into account that Rimbaud's familiarity with the poetry of Villon may be the main motive behind his peculiar orthography. Many words in Villon's fifteenth century French vocabulary are spelled with -l's instead of the -u's of modern French—*fol* rather than *fou,* for example—and these must remind one that perhaps Rimbaud was practising a kind of antique spelling that reflected or suited his Villonesque mood.

The letters of
HART CRANE

(This selection of Hart Crane's letters covers a period of approximately ten years, from 1916 when Crane was seventeen years old, to 1926 when he was twenty-seven, a period during which he wrote most of the poetry for which he is known. Crane was born in Ohio in 1899, and the first letter here is one written from Cleveland to a young painter and friend named Carl Schmitt, somewhat older than Crane, who had gone to New York City, where Crane himself was soon to live.)

To CARL SCHMITT   *CLEVELAND, NOVEMBER, 1916.*

With pipe, solitude and puppy for company, I am feeling resplendent. After a day's work in a picture store selling mezzotints and prints, you may not think it, yet there comes a great peaceful exaltation in merely reading, thinking, and writing. For occasionally in this disturbing age of adolescence which I am now undergoing, there come minutes of calm happiness and satisfaction.

I don't know whether or not I informed you in my last letter of the step, mother and I have taken. Next week mother files petition in court for her divorce from father. In this I am supporting her. So the first thing to do was to secure some employment. Your poet is now become a salesman, and (it might be worse) a job at selling pictures at Korner & Woods has been accepted.

I have had tremendous struggles, but out of the travail, I think, must come advancement. Working evenings will give me time for composing. And even should it not, I have been christened, I think, and am more or less contented with anything. Carl, I feel a great peace; my inner life has balanced, as I expected, the other side of the scale. Thank God, I am young. I have the confidence and will to *make* fate. Someday, perhaps next summer, I shall come to you and we may work together. You understand, I know.

Crane left for New York City in December and on New Year's Eve day wrote his father, a businessman in Cleveland.

To HIS FATHER   *N.Y.C. DECEMBER 31, 1916.*

My dear Father: I have just been out for a long ride up Fifth Ave. on an omnibus. It is very cold but clear, and the marble facades of the marvelous mansions shone like crystal in the sun. Carl has been very good to me, giving hours of time to me, advising, helping me get a room, etc. The room I have now is a bit too small, so after my week is up, I shall seek out another place near here, for I like the neighborhood. The houses are so different here, that it seems most interesting, for a while at least, to live in one.

It is a great shock, but a good tonic, to come down here as I have and view the countless multitudes. It seems sometimes almost as though you had lost yourself, and were trying vainly to find somewhere in this sea of humanity, your lost identity.

Today, and the remainder of the week, I shall devote to serious efforts in my writing. If you will help me to the necessities, I think that within six months I shall be fairly able to stand on my own feet.

Another letter to his father followed a few days later.

To HIS FATHER   *N.Y.C. JANUARY 5, 1917.*

My dear Father: It does me a great deal of good to hear from you often, and I hope you will continue to write me as often as you have lately done. While I am not home-sick, I yet am far from comfortable without letters, and often, from you.

Nearly every evening since my advent, has been spent in the companionship of Carl. Last night we unpacked some furniture of his which had arrived from his home, and afterward talked until twelve, or after, behind our pipes. He has some very splendid ideas about artistic, and psychic balance, analysis, etc. I realize more entirely every law, that I am preparing for a fine life: that I have powers, which, if correctly balanced, will enable me to mount to extraordinary latitudes. There is constantly an inward struggle, but the time to worry is only when there is no inward debate, and consequently there is smooth sliding to the devil. There is only one harmony, that is the equilibrium maintained by two opposite forces, equally strong. When I perceive one emotion growing overpowering to a fact, or statement of reason, then the only manly, worthy, sensible thing to do, is build up the logical side, and attain balance, and in art,— formal expression. I intend this week to begin my studying—Latin, German, and philosophy, right here in my room. They will balance my emotional nature, and lead me to more exact expression.

Two and a half years later Crane wrote from New York to one of the few friends he had made during his high school days in Ohio, a young man named William Wright, who also wished to be a poet but at the same time, unlike Crane, was continuing his formal education.

To WILLIAM WRIGHT   *N.Y.C. JUNE 17, 1919.*

Illusions are falling away from everything I look at lately. At present the world takes on the look of a desert,—a devastation to my eyes, and I am finding it rather hard at best. Still there is something of a satisfaction in the development of one's consciousness even though it is painful. There is a certain freedom gained,—a lot of things pass out of one's concern that before mattered a great deal. One feels more freedom and the result is not by any means predominantly negative. To one in my situation N.Y. is a series of exposures intense and rather savage which never would be quite as available in Cleveland, etc. New York handles one roughly but presents also more remedial recess,—more entrancing vistas than any other American location I know of. When you come to Columbia you will not be apt to feel it because any college (less Columbia than any other) enforces its own cloistral limitations which are the best things in the world while one is there. It will only be after you have left the place and lived and worked in the city (should you do so) that you will begin to feel what I mentioned.

By 1920 Crane had returned to Cleveland and worked first in his father's business, then as an advertising copywriter, to support himself while continuing to write poetry. In his letters he maintained contact with friends he had made in the literary world of New York, especially with one, Gorham Munson, a young writer better known than Crane at that time, for whom he described life in Cleveland and gave explanations of some of the poems he was writing. Two of these letters follow.

To GORHAM MUNSON   *CLEVELAND, MARCH 6, 1920.*

. . . . last night was made enjoyable by the spectacle of a good prizefight. I have been to a number lately as guest of a newspaper man who lived over at the rooming house. Of course many matches are boresome, but provide two sublime machines of human muscle-play in the vivid light of a "ring,"—stark darkness all around with yells from all sides and countless eyes gleaming, centered on the circle,—and I get a real satisfaction and stimulant. I get very heated, and shout loudly, jump from my seat, and get more interested every time I go. Really, you must attend a bout or two in N.Y. where a real knock-out is permitted. Along with liquor, that aristocratic assertion has disappeared here. There is something about the atmosphere of a ring show that I have for long wanted to capture into the snares of a poem. I shall not rest until I do, I fear. To describe it to you,— what I mean,—would be to accomplish my purpose. A kind of patent-leather gloss, an extreme freshness that has nothing to do with the traditional 'dew on the grass' variety conveys something suggestive of my aim. T.S. Eliot does it often,—once merely with the name "Sweeney," and Sherwood Anderson. . . .

To GORHAM MUNSON   *CLEVELAND, MAY, 1921.*

Dear Gorham: Excuse by apparent evasion of your request for an explanation about "Black Tambourine." The word "mid-kingdom" is perhaps the key word to what ideas there are in it. The poem is a description and bundle of insinuations, suggestions bearing on the Negro's place somewhere between man and beast. That is why Aesop is brought in, etc.—the popular conception of Negro romance, the tambourine on the wall. The value of the poem is only, to me, in what a painter would call its "tactile" quality,—an entirely aesthetic feature. A propagandist for either side of the Negro question could find anything he wanted to in it. My only declaration in it is that I find the Negro (in the popular mind) sentimentally or brutally "placed" in this mid-kingdom. Tell me if I have made it plain or not to you.

Crane also wrote from Cleveland to his friend, William Wright, now a student at Columbia University.

To WILLIAM WRIGHT *CLEVELAND, OCTOBER 17, 1921.*

. . . . if my work seems needlessly sophisticated it is because I am only interested in adding what seems to be something really *new* to what *has* been written. Unless one has some new, intensely personal viewpoint to record, say on the eternal feelings of love, and the suitable personal idiom to employ in the act, I say, why write about it? Nine chances

49

out of ten, if you know where in the past to look, you will find words already written in the more-or-less exact tongue of your soul. And the complaint to be made against nine out of ten poets is just this,—that you are apt to find their sentiments much better expressed perhaps four hundred years past. . . .

I admit to a slight leaning toward the esoteric, and am perhaps not to be taken seriously. I am fond of things of great fragility, and also and especially of the kind of poetry John Donne represents, a dark, musky, brooding, speculative vintage, at once sensual and spiritual, and singing rather the beauty of experience than innocence.

As you did not "get" my idiom in "Chaplinesque," I feel rather like doing my best to explain myself. I am moved to put Chaplin with the poets (of today); hence the "we." In other words, he, especially in *The Kid,* made me feel myself, as a poet, as being in the same boat with him. Poetry, the human feelings, "the kitten," is so crowded out of the humdrum, rushing, mechanical scramble of today that the man who would preserve them must duck and camouflage for dear life to keep them or keep himself from annihilation. I have since learned that I am by no means alone in seeing these things in the buffooneries of the tragedian, Chaplin, and in the poem I have tried to express these 'social sympathies' in words corresponding somewhat to the antics of the actor.

Crane's concern with style in his poetry was expressed perhaps most concisely in a letter to Sherwood Anderson, whose stories he admired and whose Winesburg, Ohio *he had ecstatically reviewed for a little magazine* The Pagan, *in 1919, when the book had first appeared. This review started a correspondence between Anderson and Crane which continued for a number of years. In the summer after the letter printed here, Anderson passed through Cleveland and visited Crane. It may have been a letter of Anderson's from Alabama that inspired the poem, "Black Tambourine," of which Crane reminds him here.*

To SHERWOOD ANDERSON
CLEVELAND, JANUARY 10, 1922

Dear Anderson:
In my own work I find the problem of style and form becoming more and more difficult as time goes on. I imagine

that I am interested in this style of writing much more than you are. Perhaps, though, we include the same features under different terms. In verse this feature can become a preoccupation, to be enjoyed for its own sake. I do not think you will sympathize with me very strongly on this point, but, of course, if you got as much pleasure out of finding instances of it in other writers as I do, you would see what I mean. For instance, when I come to such a line as the following from John Donne, I am thrilled—"Thou shalt not peepe through lattices of eyes,/Nor heare through Labyrinths of eares." Or take another, called "The Expiration" . . . .[1] What I want to get is just what is so beautifully done in this poem,—an *interior* form, a form that is so thorough and intense as to dye the words themselves with a peculiarity of meaning, slightly different maybe from the ordinary definition of them separate from the poem. If you remember my "Black Tambourine" you will perhaps agree with me that I have at least accomplished this idea once. My aims make writing slow for me, and so far I have done practically nothing. . . .

The Sam Loveman mentioned by Crane in this letter of 1922 to Munson would become Crane's literary executor after Crane's death a decade later.

To GORHAM MUNSON   *CLEVELAND, JUNE 18, 1922.*

Dear Gorham: I have been in a house up in "Little Italy," a section of Sicilian immigrants very near our house where one can get good three-year Chianti,—and incidentally am feeling very fine as Sunday evenings go. *There* is the place to enjoy oneself, in the family parlour of a pickslinger's family with chromos on the walls that are right in the style of Derain and Vlaminck. Bitch dogs and the rest of the family wander in while the bottle is still half empty and some of the family offspring. *Tristram Shandy* read to a friend with a Spanish Bolero going on the Victrola sounds good in such a milieu! I never should live without wine! When you come here we shall make many visits to this

[1] Crane quoted for Anderson the opening twelve lines of this poem by Donne. The first poem from which he quotes is "The Second Anniversary," lines 297–298.

51

charming family. You will like my classic, puritan, inhibited friend Sam Loveman who translates Baudelaire charmingly! It is hard to get him to do anything outside the imagination,—but he is charming and has just given me a work on Greek vases (made in Deutschland) in which satyrs with great erections prance to the ceremonies of Dionysos with all the fervour of de Gourmont's descriptions of sexual sacrifice in *Physique de L'Amour* which I am lately reading in trans.

. . . . . At times, dear Gorham, I feel an enormous power in me—that seems almost supernatural. If this power is not too dissipated in aggravation and discouragement I may amount to something sometime.

During the Christmas holidays when his friend Wright was home from New York, in Warren, Ohio, Crane wrote him from Cleveland, describing his job with an advertising company and making some comments on American life as a whole.

To WILLIAM WRIGHT *CLEVELAND, DECEMBER 24, 1922.*

Dear William: However much boredom you may find in Warren—I assure you it will not be as strenuous as the hot water I am stewing in. The Pittsburgh Water Heater surely has been on my mind the last three weeks, and the burden is still unshifted. I am growing bald trying to scratch up new ideas in housekeeping and personal hygiene—to tell people why they need more and quicker hot water. Last night I got drunk on some sherry. Even in that wild orgy my mind was still enchained by the hot water complex, —and I sat down and reeled off the best lines written so far in my handling of the campaign. All of my poems in the future will attest this sterilizing influence of HOT WATER!

Nothing happens here, either. I am grateful only for wine. I have neither women or song. Cleveland street car rides twice a day take out all hope of these latter elements. I think of New York and next summer when the present is too sharp (or is it dull!) But the main faults are not of our city alone. They are of the age. A period that is loose at all ends, without apparent direction of any sort. In some ways the most amazing age there ever was. Appalling and dull at the same time.

In the New Year, 1923. Crane sent Munson in New York the last section of his poem, "Faustus and Helen," which he had partly composed during a visit his friend had made in Cleveland the preceding summer.

To GORHAM MUNSON   *CLEVELAND, JANUARY 14, 1923.*

Dear Gorham: This (enclosed) may, or may not yet be finished. Anyway, I think it is rounded enough as it is to be somewhat enjoyed.

Some things about it surprise and satisfy me. It has a bit of Dionysian splendor, perhaps an overtone of some of our evenings together last summer. It is so packed with tangential slants, interwoven symbolisms, that I'm not sure whether or not it will be understood. However, I am sure that it perfectly consorts with the other two parts of the poem as I intend them:

> Part I
> *Meditation, Evocation, Love, Beauty*
> Part II
> *Dance, Humor, Satisfaction*
> Part III
> *Tragedy, War (the eternal soldier), Resumé, Ecstasy, Final Declaration*

There is an organization and symphonic rhythm to III that I did not think I could do. The last three evenings have been wonderful for me, anyway! A kind of ecstasy and power for WORK.

III doesn't seem half long enough to me now—but I'm too much with and in it to know.

At this time Crane began a correspondence with Waldo Frank, one of the founders of the little magazine, The Seven Arts, *and author of an influential book of the time,* Our America, *examining the cultural and spiritual condition of the country. Frank became Crane's most trusted confidant, the "dear repository of my faith," as he would call him in a later letter. Frank would write the Introduction to Crane's Collected Poems.*

To WALDO FRANK   *CLEVELAND, FEBRUARY 27, 1923.*

Dear Waldo Frank: Such major criticism as both you and Gorham have given my "Faustus and Helen" is the most sensitizing influence I have ever encountered. It is a new feeling, and a glorious one, to have one's inmost delicate

53

intentions so fully recognized as your last letter to me attested. I can feel a calmness on the sidewalk—where before I felt a defiance only. And better than all—I am certain that a number of us at last have some kind of community of interest. And with this communion will come something better than a mere clique. It is a consciousness of something more vital than stylistic questions and 'taste', it is vision, and a vision alone that not only America needs, but the whole world. We are not sure where this will lead, but after the complete renunciation symbolized in *The Wasteland* and, though less, in *Ulysses* we have sensed some new vitality. Whether I am in that current remains to be seen, — but I am enough in it at least to be sure that you are definitely in it already. What delights me almost beyond words is that my natural idiom (which I have unavoidably stuck to in spite of nearly everybody's nodding, querulous head) has reached and carried to you so completely the very blood and bone of me. There is only one way of saying what comes to one in ecstasy. One works and works over it to finish and organize it perfectly—but fundamentally that doesn't affect one's *way* of saying it.

During his last weeks in Cleveland before returning finally to New York City, which Crane felt was the only place for him, he wrote two letters to Munson which reveal the state of high poetic excitement he was experiencing. His major poem, The Bridge, *which he first refers to here, was initially inspired by the image of the Brooklyn Bridge.*

To GORHAM MUNSON *CLEVELAND, FEBRUARY 18, 1923.*

. . . . It (*The Bridge*) is just beginning to take the least outline, —and the more outline the conception of the thing takes, the more its final difficulties appal me. All this preliminary thought has to result, of course, in some channel forms or mould into which I throw myself at white heat. Very roughly, it concerns a mystical synthesis of "America." History and fact, location, etc., all have to be transfigured into abstract form that would almost function independently of its subject matter. The initial impulses of "our people" will have to be gathered up toward the climax of the bridge, symbol of our constructive future, our unique identity, in which is included also our scientific hopes and achievements of the future. The mystic portent of all this is already flocking through my mind (when I say this I should say "the mystic possibilities," but that is all that's worth announcing, anyway) but the actual statement of the thing, the marshalling of the forces, will take me months, at best; and I may have to give it up entirely before that; it may be too impossible an ambition. But if I do succeed, such a waving of banners, such ascent of towers, such dancing, will never before have been put down on paper! The form will be symphonic, something like "F and H" with its treatment of varied content . . . . I am grateful for your very rich suggestions best stated in your (Waldo) *Frank Study* on the treatment of mechanical manifestations of today as subject for lyrical, dramatic, and even epic poetry. You must already notice that influence in "F and H." It is to figure even larger in *The Bridge*. The field of possibilities literally glitters all around one with the perception and vocabulary to pick out significant details and digest them into something emotional.

To GORHAM MUNSON   *CLEVELAND, MARCH 2, 1923.*

Dear Gorham: The last several days have been equally among the most intense in my life. The annoyance comes in only on the swing of a repressive *fate.* To be stimulated to the *nth* degree with your head burgeoning with ideas and conceptions of the most baffling interest and lure—and then to have to munch ideas on water heaters (I am writing another book for house fraus!) has been a real cruelty this time, however temporary. The more I think about my *Bridge* poem the more thrilling its symbolical possibilities become, and since my reading of you and Frank (I recently bought *City Block*) I begin to feel myself directly connected with Whitman. I feel myself in currents that are positively awesome in their extent and possibilities. "Faustus and Helen" was only a beginning—but in it I struck new *timbres* that suggest dozens more, all unique, yet poignant and expressive of our epoch. Modern music almost drives me crazy! I went to hear D'Indy's *II Symphony* last night and my hair stood on end at its revelations. To get those, and others of men like Strauss, Ravel, Scriabin, and Bloch into *words*, one needs to ransack the vocabularies of Shakespeare, Jonson, Webster (for theirs are the richest) and add

and accident not to think about you and your situation many hours. What the details of those matters were certainly would not help me to realize any the better that you have been going through a very tumultous period and that it has been very fortunate that you should arrive in the country when you did, not that you escaped them, —but that you were able to *see* them more tranquilly. The city is a place of "brokenness," of drama; but when a certain development in this intensity is reached a new stage is created, or must be, arbitrarily, or there is a foreshortening, a loss and a premature disintegration of experience. You are setting the keynote now for a higher tranquility than ever. It is an even wider intensity, also. You see, I am writing to you perhaps very egotistically, but you will understand that I am always seeing your life and experience very solidly as a part of my own because I feel our identities so much alike in spiritual direction. When it comes to action we diverge in several ways, —but I'm sure we center in common devotions, in a kind of timeless vision.

In the above sense I feel you as entering very strongly into certain developments in *The Bridge*. May I say it, and not seem absurd, that you are the first, or rather the purest living indice of a new order of consciousness that I have met? We are accomplices in many ways that we don't yet fully understand. "What is now proved was once only imagined," said Blake. I have to combat every day those really sincere people, but limited, who deny the superior logic of metaphor in favor of their perfect sums, divisions and subtractions. They cannot go a foot unless to merely catch up with some predetermined and set boundaries, nor can they realize that they do nothing but walk ably over an old track bedecked with all kinds of signposts and "championship records." Nobody minds their efforts, which frequently amount to a great deal, —but I object to their system of judgment being so regally applied to what I'm interested in doing. Such a cramping cannot be reconciled with the work which you have done, and which I feel myself a little beginning to do. The great energies about us cannot be transformed that way into a higher quality of life, and by perfecting our sensibilities, response and actions, we are always contributing more than we can realize (rationalise) at the time. We answer them a little vaguely, first, because our ends are forever unaccomplished, and because, secondly, our work is self-explanatory enough, if they could "see" it. I nearly go mad with the intense but always misty realization of what *can* be done if potentialities are fully freed, released. I know you to feel the same way about your camera, —despite all that you actually *have* done with it already. In that sense I hope to make it the one memorable thing to you in this letter that I think you should go on with your photographic synthesis of life this summer and fall, gathering together those dangerous interests outside of yourself into that purer projection of yourself. It is really not a projection in any but a loose sense, for I feel more and more that in the absolute sense the artist *identifies* himself with life. Because he has always had so much surrounding indifference and resistance such "action" takes on a more relative and limited term which has been abused and misunderstood by several generations, —this same "projecting." But in the true mystical sense as well as in the sense which Aristotle meant by the "imitation of nature," I feel that I'm right.

I shall go on thinking of you, the apples and the gable, and writing you whenever I can get a moment. So much has to be crammed into my narrow evenings and holidays, that I am becoming a poor correspondent with everyone, I fear. You will realize how much I am with you, I feel sure, by other signs. I am sending you a roughly typed sheet containing some lines from *The Bridge*. They symbolize its main intentions. However, as they are fragmentary and not in entirely finished form, please don't show them around. I only want you to get a better idea of what I'm saying than could be "said" in prose. Some of the lines will be clear enough to give a glimpse of some of my ideas whether or not the Whole can be grasped from such fragments or not. . . .

To ALFRED STIEGLITZ   *N.Y.C. AUGUST 25, 1923.*

Dear Stieglitz: I am hoping that you have seen Waldo, as you mentioned in your letter, by this time. The idea seemed so sensible to me, knowing as I have, the uneasy frictions that have bothered both of you and having regretted so much the evident misunderstandings all around. It is very important for us all—that is, all who are trying to establish an honest basis for what work we get a chance to do. It isn't, as you say, a matter of politics, —but something akin to our spiritual bread and butter. No all our manna comes from the skies. And we suffer all too much from social malnutrition once we try to live *entirely* with the ghostly past. We must somehow touch the clearest veins of eternity flowing through the crowds around us—or risk being the kind of glorious cripples that have missed some vital part of their inheritance.

It's good to hear that you have been "at the camera" again and that you are recovering, with physical and nervous rest, that extremity of delicate equilibrium that goes into your best activities. I know what it is to be exiled for months at a time. They're the usual things with me, and lately it has been especially hard to be cut up between the necessities of a readjustment at the office (they've put me into a new department and I enjoy writing copy again to some extent) and the more natural propulsion toward such things as *The Bridge*. I've been in such despair about this latter for some time! —not seeing my way to introduce it in the way I want (the end and climax, what you have seen, is all that's done so far) and not getting the needful hours to ripen anything in myself. If I can once get certain obligations disposed of in my family, I shall certainly break loose and do only such simple labor for my room and board as will not come into my consciousness after "working hours." Streams of "copy" and ad layouts course through my head all night sometimes until I feel like a thread singed and twisted in the morning. This has been, very likely, as strenuous a year and as wasteful a one as I shall encounter for a long time, although you can never foretell such things as long as you have a family and connections. But I am looking forward to a more equable program when winter comes, when people's windows are shut, cats are quieter and the air more bracing.

Every once in a while I get a statement or so noted down in regard to my interpretation of you and your photographs. There are still many things in the lucid explanation of them that simply baffle me. To use a modern simile that occurred to me in that connection—it's like trying to locate "the wires of the Acropolis"; indeed, I may call my essay by that name before I get through. . . .

Two other artist friends of Crane's, less well known than Stieg-litz, were William Sommers and Richard Rychtarik, whom he had met in Cleveland and with whom he frequently corres-ponded from New York. Sommers was a man fifty years old who worked for a living as a lithographer in a printing com-pany; despite Crane's efforts to show Sommer's paintings to influential writers and critics in the New York art world, Som-mers remained quite obscure. Rychartik, a Czechoslovakian from Prague, achieved success as a theatrical designer, doing sets for the Metropolitan Opera, and eventually settling in New York. Crane had formed an especially warm friendship with Rychartik's wife, Charlotte, and often wrote his letters to her.

To WILLIAM SOMMERS   *N.Y.C. MAY 9, 1923.*

. . . . in almost every way, N.Y. is getting to be a really stupendous place. It is the center of the world today, as Alexandria became the nucleus of another older civili-zation. The wealthier and upper parts of the city have their own beauty, but I prefer as a steady thing the wonderful streets of this lower section, crowded with life, packed with movement and drama, children, kind and drab-looking women, elbows braced on window ledges, and rows of vege-tables lining the streets that you would love to paint. Life is possible here at greater intensity than probably any other place in the world today. . . .

To CHARLOTTE RYCHTARIK   *N.Y.C. JULY 21, 1923.*

. . . I have just come back from a lonely meal in Prince Street, —the place where Richard ate with me, and where I have been many times since he left. Ah, yes, there is wine, but what is wine when you drink it alone! Yet, I am happy here in my room with the Victrola playing Ravel, —the Faery Garden piece which you and I heard so often to-gether up in my room in Cleveland. When I think of that room, it is almost to give way to tears, because I shall never find my way back to it. It is not necessary, of course, that I should, but just the same it was the center and beginning of all that I am and ever will be, the center of such pain as would tear me to pieces to tell you about, and equally the center of great joys! *The Bridge* seems to me so beautiful, —and it was there that I first thought about it, and it was there that I wrote "Faustus and Helen". . . .

In the winter of 1923, while Crane was staying with his friend, the writer, Slater Brown, in Woodstock, N.Y. he met Gaston Lachaise, the sculptor, for whom he wrote a poem.[1] Lachaise, in return, made a white sea gull for Crane.[2]

To ISABEL *and* GASTON LACHAISE *N.Y.C. JANUARY 9, 1924.*

Dear Mme. and Gaston! There are no memories stronger than the spiritual outlines of rock and branch so bare and fine as winter mountains yielded me while I was with you and two precious others recently. So, in a moment of enthusiasm for all things great I must inscribe a greeting and regret (thus floridly!) that we can't presently walk and talk "all together." And as a sort of apology, offer the enclosed poem to your appreciation. . . . Especially do I send it—because I feel it had its first thought in the dance of music, flesh and stone wherein you live always—you two!

In the midst of Crane's letters to his friends, there appears from time to time a letter to his father, to whom he had expressed his early enthusiasms on his first trip to New York. Since that time, because of various disturbances, principally his mother's and father's divorce, communication between Crane and his father had grown increasingly strained and more difficult, though both of them evidently desired to maintain it. The following letter was written by Crane to his father after a break of more than two years virtually without communication between them—when both were again making efforts to reestablish the relationship.

[1] This poem, titled "Interludium," is not found in Crane's *Collected Poems,* but was printed by Brom Weber in the Appendix to his *Hart Crane,* New York, 1948.

[2] In a letter of Feb. 10th, 1926, from Patterson, New York, and a postcard from the Isle of Pines in August of the same year, Crane refers to this gull by Lachaise. "Constantly your seagull has floated in my mind, ever since I saw it . . ." "Your bird (the gull) is divine, produces sea music, even winks at times!" Crane means divine in the original sense—as being a kind of God. The seagull has its manifestation in Crane's poetry in Proem: To Brooklyn Bridge, "Then, with inviolate curve, forsake our eyes/As apparitional as sails that cross/Some page of figures to be filed away."

My dear Father: . . . . You are a very busy man these days as I well appreciate from the details in your letter, and I have perhaps bored you with these explanations about myself, your sympathies engaged as they are—so much in other activities, and your mind filled with a thousand and one details and obligations which clamour to be fulfilled. Nevertheless, as I've said before, I couldn't see any other way than to frankly tell you about myself and my interests so as not to leave any accidental afterthought in your mind that I had any "personal" reasons for not working in the Crane Company. And in closing I would like to just ask you to think some time, —try to imagine working for the pure love of simply making something beautiful, —something that maybe can't be sold or used to help sell anything else, but that is simply a communication between man and man, a bond of understanding and human enlightenment—which is what a real work of art *is*. If you do that, then maybe you will see why I am not so foolish after all to have followed what seems sometimes only a faint star. I only ask to leave behind me something that the future may find valuable, and it takes a bit of sacrifice sometimes in order to give the thing that you know is in yourself and worth giving. I shall make every sacrifice toward that end.

A large number of Crane's letters were to his mother and maternal grandmother. A group of these, written from Brooklyn Heights where Crane lived during most of 1924, with a splendid view of the Bridge that inspired the long poem he was composing, are printed together here.

To HIS MOTHER *and* GRANDMOTHER
                              BROOKLYN, MAY 11, 1924.

Dear Grace and Grandma: I am told that this section of Brooklyn around here (Brooklyn Heights) is very much like London. Certainly it is very quiet and charming, with its many old houses and all a little different, and with occasional trees jutting up an early green through the pavements. I have just come back from breakfast and saw some tulips dotting the edge of one of the several beautiful garden patches that edge the embankment that leads down to the river. It certainly is refreshing to live in such a neighborhood, and even though I should not succeed in acquiring a room that actually commands the harbor view I think I shall always want to live in this section anyway. Mr. ———, who has such a back room in this house, has invited me to use his room whenever he is out, and the other evening the view from his window was one never to be forgotten. Everytime one looks at the harbor and the NY skyline across the river it is quite different, and the range of atmospheric effects is endless. But at twilight on a foggy evening, such as it was at this time, it is beyond description. Gradually the lights in the enormously tall buildings begin to flicker through the mist. There was a great cloud enveloping the top of the Woolworth tower, while below, in the river, were streaming reflections of myriad lights, continually being crossed by the twinkling mast and deck lights of little tugs scudding along, freight rafts, and occasional liners starting outward. Look far to your left toward Staten Island and there is the Statue of Liberty, with that remarkable lamp of hers that makes her seen for miles. And up at the right Brooklyn Bridge, the most superb piece of construction in the modern world, I'm sure, with strings of light crossing it like glowing worms as the L's and surface cars pass each other going and coming. It is particularly fine to feel the greatest city in the world from enough distance, as I do here, to see its larger proportions. When you are actually in it you are often too distracted to realize its better and more imposing aspects. Yes, this location is the best one on all counts for me. For the first time in many weeks I am beginning to further elaborate my plans for my *Bridge* poem. . . .

To HIS MOTHER *and* GRANDMOTHER
BROOKLYN, OCTOBER 21, 1924.

Dear Grace and Grandma: The last day of my vacation, and somehow the best! So cold and sharp it is, you might think it time for turkey. You know how keenly brilliant the atmosphere around these parts can be—frequently in any season. On such days one gets an even better edge to this glorious light here by the harbor. The water so very blue, the foam and steam from the tugs so dazzlingly white! I like the liners best that are painted white—with red and black funnels like those United Fruit boats across the river, standing at rest. And you should see the lovely plumes of steam

64

that issue from the enormous height of skyscrapers across the way. I've been toasting my feet at an electric stove, a kind of radio heater that I have in my room, and glancing first at the bay, then with another kind of satisfaction at my shelves of books and writing table, —for a long time unable to think of anything but a kind of keen sensual bliss, that is in itself something like action—it contains so much excitement and pleasure.

To HIS MOTHER   *BROOKLYN, NOVEMBER 16, 1924.*

Dear Grace: . . . . It darkened before five today and the wind's onslaught across the bay turns up white-caps in the river's mouth. The gulls are chilly-looking creatures—constantly wheeling around in search of food here in the river as they do hundreds of miles out at sea in the wakes of liners. The radiator sizzles in the room here and it is warm enough for anyone's comfort, even yours. I feel as though I were well arranged for a winter of rich work, reading and excitement—there simply isn't half time enough (that's my main complaint) for all that is offered. And the weeks go by so fast! . . . .

My—but how the wind is blowing. Rain, too, on the window now! There was a wonderful fog for about 18 hours last week. One couldn't even see the garden close behind the house—to say nothing of the piers. All night long there were distant tinklings, buoy bells and siren warnings from river craft. It was like wakening into a dreamland in the early dawn—one wondered where one was with only a milky light in the window and that vague music from a hidden world. Next morning while I dressed it was clear and glittering as usual. Like champagne, or a cold bath to look at it. Such a world!

It was to Waldo Frank, however, that Crane confided the most penetrating description of his sexual and poetic experience at this time. In the following letter, Columbia Heights is another name for Brooklyn Heights.

To WALDO FRANK   *BROOKLYN, APRIL 21, 1924.*

Dear Waldo: For many days, now, I have gone about quite dumb with something for which "happiness" must be too

65

mild a term. At any rate, my aptitude for communication, such as it ever is!, has been limited to one person alone, and perhaps for the first time in my life (and, I can only think that it is for the last, so far is my imagination from the conception of anything more profound and lovely than this love). I have wanted to write you more than once, but it will take many letters to let you know what I mean (for myself, at least) when I say that I have seen the Word made Flesh. I mean nothing less, and I known now that there is such a thing as indestructibility. In the deepest sense, where flesh became transformed through intensity of response to counter-response, where sex was beaten out, where a purity of joy was reached that included tears. It's true, Waldo, that so much more than my frustrations and multitude of humiliations has been answered in this reality and promise that I feel that whatever event the future holds is justified beforehand. And I have been able to give freedom and life which was acknowledged in the ecstasy of walking hand in hand across the most beautiful bridge of the world, the cables enclosing us and pulling us upward in such a dance as I have never walked and never can walk with another.

Note the above address (110 Columbia Heights), and you will see that I am living in the shadow of that bridge. It is so quiet here; in fact, it's like the moment of the communion with the "religious gunman" in my "F and H" where the edge of the bridge leaps over the edge of the street. It was in the evening darkness of its shadow that I started the last part of that poem. Imagine my surprise when E— brought me to this street where, at the very end of it, I saw a scene that was more familiar than a hundred factual previsions could have rendered it! And there is all the glorious dance of the river directly beyond the back window of the room I am to have as soon as E—'s father moves out, which is to be soon. E— will be back then from S. America where he had to ship for wages as ship's writer. That window is where I would be most remembered of all: the ships, the harbor, and the skyline of Manhattan, midnight, morning or evening, —rain, snow or sun, it is everything from mountains to the walls of Jerusalem and Nineveh, and all related and in actual contact with the changelessness of the many waters that surround it. I think the sea has thrown itself upon me and been answered, at least in

66

part, and I believe I am a little changed—not essentially, but changed and transubstantiated as anyone is who has asked a question and been answered.

Now I can thank you for the wisdom of your last letter to me, and most of all for your confidence in me. (It is strange, but I can feel no place for paragraphs in this letter!) (Yet one goes on making paragraphs.) It came at the very moment of my present understanding, and it is as though it, in some clairvoyant way, included it. Only, I so much wish you were here these days for you are the only one I know who quite encircles my experience. I shall never, of course, be able to give any account of it to anyone in direct terms, but you will be here and not so far from now. Then we shall take a walk across the bridge to Brooklyn (as well as to Estador, for all that!). Just now I feel the flood tide again the way it seemed to me just before I left Cleveland last year, and I feel like slapping you on the back every half-hour.

During the winter of 1925 and spring of 1926 Crane was sharing a house in Patterson, N.Y. with Allen Tate and his wife, until an unfortunate incident broke up the arrangement. Crane also came to a parting of the ways with his old friend, Gorham Munson, over a critique of Crane's poetry in which Crane thought Munson showed a failure to understand the very nature of the poet's art. Following is a passage from a letter of Crane's to Munson that states Crane's own conception.

To GORHAM MUNSON *PATTERSON, N. Y. MARCH 17, 1926.*

What you admire in Plato as "divine sanity" is the architecture of his logic. Plato doesn't live today because of the instrinsic "truth" of his statements: their only living truth today consists in the "fact" of their harmonious relationship to each other in the context of his organization of them. This grace partakes of poetry. But Plato was primarily a philosopher, and you must admit that grace is a secondary motive in philosophical statement, at least until the hypothetical basis of an initial "truth" has been accepted— not in the name of beauty, form or experience, but in the name of rationality. No wonder Plato considered the banishment of poets; —their reorganizations of chaos on a basis perhaps divergent from his own threatened the logic of *his* system, itself founded on assumptions that demanded the very defense of poetic construction which he was fortunately able to provide.

The tragic quandary (or *argon*) of the modern world derives from the paradoxes that an inadequate system of rationality forces on the living consciousness. I am not opposing any new synthesis of reasonable laws which might provide a consistent philosophical and moral program for our epoch. Neither, on the other hand, am I attempting through poetry to delineate any such system. If this "knowledge," as you call it, were so sufficiently organized as to dominate the limitations of my personal experience (consciousness) then I would probably find myself automatically writing under its "classic" power of dictation, and under that circumstance might be incidentally as philosophically "contained" as you might wish me to be. That would mean "serenity" to you because the abstract basis of my work would have been familiarized to you before you read a word of the poetry. But my poetry, even then, —in so far as it was truly poetic, —would avoid the employment of abstract tags, formulations of experience in factual terms, etc. —it would necessarily express its concepts in the more direct terms of physical-psychic experience. If not, it must by so much lose its impact and become simply categorical.

At the end of April, Crane in company with Waldo Frank sailed from New York City to Havana, Cuba, and thence to the Isle of Pines where Crane's family had long owned a sort of vacation house that Crane had visited as a boy. The house had been neglected for years and was lived in by an old housekeeper named Mrs. Simpson, with whom Crane became great friends and who appears in several of his last poems. Crane had come there to work on The Bridge, *which had been going rather slowly. After a month or so, Frank left him by himself, returning to New York, where Crane wrote him describing his progress on the poem.*

To WALDO FRANK   *ISLE OF PINES, JUNE 20, 1926.*

The form of my poem rises out of a past that so overwhelms the present with its worth and vision that I'm at a loss to explain my delusion that there exist any real links between that past and a future destiny worthy of it. The "destiny" is long since completed, perhaps the little last section of my poem is a hangover echo of it—but it hangs suspended somewhere in ether like an Absalom by his hair. The bridge as a symbol today has no significance beyond an economical approach to shorter hours, quicker lunches, behaviorism and toothpicks. And inasmuch as the bridge is a symbol of all such poetry as I am interested in writing it is my present fancy that a year from now I'll be more contented working in an office than before. Rimbaud was the last great poet that our civilization will see—he let off all the great cannon crackers in Vahalla's parapets, the sun has set theatrically several times since while Laforgue, Eliot and others of that kidney have whimpered fastidiously. *Everybody* writes poetry now—and "poets" for the first time are about to receive official social and economic recognition in America. It's really all the fashion, but a dead bore to anticipate. If only America were half as worthy today to be spoken of as Whitman spoke of it fifty years ago there might be something for me to say—not that Whitman received or required any tangible proof of his intimations, but that time has shown how increasingly lonely and ineffectual his confidence stands.

There always remains the cult of "words," elegancies, elaborations, to exhibit with a certain amount of pride to an "inner circle" of literary initiates. But this is, to me, rivalled by numerous other forms of social accomplishment which might, if attained, provide as mild and seductive recognitions. . . .

To WALDO FRANK   *ISLE OF PINES, AUGUST 19, 1926.*

Dear Waldo: Here, too, is that bird with a note that Rimbaud speaks of as "making you blush."[1] We are in the midst of the equatorial storm season; everyday, often at night, torrents engulf us, and the thunder rods jab and prospect in the caverns deep below that chain of mountains across. You can hear the very snakes rejoice, —the long, shaken-out convulsions of rock and roots.

It is very pleasant to lie awake—just half awake—and listen. I have the most speechless and glorious dreams meanwhile. Sometimes words come and go, presented like a rose that yields only its light, never its composite form.

[1] Crane is referring to a passage from Rimbaud's prose poem, "Enfance III," in *Les Illuminations.* "Au bois il y a un oiseau, son chant vous arrête et vous fait rougir."

Then the cocks begin to crow. I hear Mrs. S— begin to stir. She is the very elf of music, little wrinkled burnous wisp that can do anything and remembers so much! She reads Dante and falls to sleep, her cough has become so admirably imitated by the parrot that I often think her in two places at once.

I have made up a kind of friendship with that idiot boy, who is always on the road when I come into town for mail. He has gone so far as to answer my salutations. I was unexpected witness one day of the most astonishing spectacle; not that I was surprised. A group of screaming children were shrieking about in a circle. I looked toward the house and saw the boy standing mostly hid behind the wooden shutters behind the grating; his huge limp phallus waved out at them from some opening; the only other part visible was his head, in a most gleeful grin, swaying above the lower division of the blinds.

When I saw him next he was talking to a blue little kite high in the afternoon. He is rendingly beautiful at times: I have encountered him in the road, talking again tout seul and examining pebbles and cinders and marble chips through the telescope of a twice-opened tomato can. He is very shy, hilarious, —and undoubtedly idiot. I have been surprised to notice how much the other children like him.

I'm glad to know that *The Bridge* is fulfilling your utmost intuitions; for an intuition it undoubtedly was. You didn't need to tell me that you had "seen" something that memorable evening, although I was never so sure just what it was you saw, until now. But I have always carried that peculiar look that was in your eyes for a moment there in your room; it has often recurred in my thoughts. What I should have done without your love and most distinguished understanding is hard to say, but there is no earthly benefit for which I would exchange it. It is a harmony always with the absolute direction I always seek, often miss, but sometimes gain.

The Bridge *was virtually completed during the six months that Crane remained on the Isle of Pines. By September he was already contemplating another long work which he described to Frank as "a blank verse tragedy of Aztec mythology—for which I shall have to study the obscure calendars of dead kings."*

Crane never actually composed any part of this projected work, though he later received a Guggenheim Fellowship which took him to Mexico. There are a number of shorter poems written during and after the final stages of his composition of The Bridge, *among them "The Idiot," a poem inspired by the idiot boy on the Isle of Pines whom he described in the letter to Frank printed above. But after the completion of* The Bridge *Crane's achievement in poetry had reached its climax. On his return from Mexico in 1932, bound again for New York, he jumped overboard into the sea off the coast of Cuba. He was thirty-two years old.*

750 copies of the second impression of this book have been printed in Times New Roman type by the Printing Division of The University of Texas.
Design and typography by Kim Taylor